Run Home & Take a Bow

Run Home & Take a Bow

STORIES OF LIFE, FAITH, AND A SEASON WITH THE KANSAS CITY ROYALS

Ethan D. Bryan

With
Les Norman
Kevin Seitzer
&
The 2011 KC Royals

A Division of Samizdat
Publishing Group

SAMIZDAT CREATIVE
A Division of Samizdat Publishing Group, LLC.
Golden, Colorado 80401

Run Home and Take a Bow. Copyright © 2012 by Ethan D. Bryan. All rights reserved. Printed in the United States of America. No part of this book may be used or reproduced in any manner whatsoever without written permission except in the case of brief quotations embodied in critical articles and reviews. For information, email comrade@samizdatcreative.com.

The author can be reached at runhomebook.com.

ISBN: 978-1-938633-00-3

Library of Congress Cataloging-in-Publication Data is available upon request.

Samizdat Creative books may be purchased with bulk discounts for educational, business, or sales promotional use. For information please email: comrade@samizdatcreative.com

Samizdat Creative online: samizdatcreative.com

Cover Design: Brett Kesinger

Scripture quotations in this publication are taken from the Holy Bible, New International Version® (NIV®). Copyright © 1973, 1978, 1984 by International Bible Society. Used by permission of Zondervan. All rights reserved; the New American Standard Bible® (NASB), Copyright © 1960, 1962, 1963, 1968, 1971, 1972, 1973, 1975, 1977, 1995 by The Lockman Foundation. Used by permission; the Amplified Bible (AMP), © The Lockman Foundation 1954, 1958, 1962, 1964, 1965, 1987; The Living Bible (TLB), copyright © 1971, used by permission of Tyndale House Publishers, Inc., Wheaton, IL 60189, all rights reserved; and the King James Version (KJV).

Contents

Introduction. 9
Opening Day. 13
Baseball is Beautiful. 21
Never Give Up. 28
The View from My Seat. 34
Play Ball. 41
Civil Disagreements. 49
If At First You Succeed. 58
It's All About the Numbers? 66
The Big Picture. 73
Remembering 82
Baseball Is for Friends. 91
Sophie's Questions 98

The Transformations of Alex Gordon and
Kaylea Bryan 105

Major League Lessons: Kevin Seitzer................ 114

Buck O'Neil Day................................. 120

Major League Lessons: Les Norman 129

The Next Generation............................. 137

Sacred Time..................................... 145

Weathering the Storm 152

Take a Bow 160

Run Home 167

Save the Best for Last 176

Box Scores...................................... 183

*To Jamie, Kaylea, and Sophie,
You are my everyday heroes — take a bow.*

*To Kevin, Les, and Alex,
Thanks for sharing your stories
and love of the game with me.*

*To those who dream of playing
just one more game,*

I'll see you at the ballpark. Bring a glove.

Introduction

Baseball is the language of my soul.

My love of baseball goes back further than I can possibly remember. Growing up, I avidly collected baseball cards and players' autographs, following the statistics of my favorite players every morning in the sports page. I listened to Royals on Radio broadcasts every night while I tried to fall asleep.

Chuck E. Cheese sponsored my first baseball team. We wore red pants with tall socks and a mesh hat that made my ears stick out sideways—dotting my bald head with funny tan lines. Toward the end of the season I pitched in my first game. That day on that "flat mound" I discovered a part of myself. Starting that summer and continuing daily for years, I waited for Dad to come home so we could play catch as soon as he stepped out of his car.

I played ball competitively through my sophomore year in high school. After that summer's legion season, I hung up my spikes. My last at-bat was a fly out to the warning track. A part of my soul went into mourning that day. Up until that point, my lifelong dream had been to play baseball for the Kansas City Royals. I was now quitting on my dream. I had yet to hit my growth spurt, topping the scales at a lean 110 pounds. I was easily the smallest guy on the team. That was 1991. For the next decade, I completely tuned out of baseball and plunged myself into playing golf.

Success in golf came quickly. I competed in the state tournament my junior and senior years of high school. I was the co-champion of our conference tournament, shooting a solid even par round. I loved playing golf with Dad and family and friends. At that time, I thought that my love for golf would supersede my love for baseball.

I was wrong.

Ten years after quitting baseball, I moved to Kansas City with my wife, Jamie, and our newborn daughter, Kaylea Grace. I had just graduated from George W. Truett Theological Seminary at Baylor University and was hired by a young church to lead worship and work with the youth. The church was an answer to prayer. As part of the job interview, Jamie and I attended a Royals game. The Royals won in the bottom of the 13th inning on a Mike Sweeney home run. I took it as a sign from above.

My passion for the game and the boys in blue returned almost immediately. Friends and church members would occasionally offer me free tickets, especially as the seasons moved into August and September and the Royals weren't in contention for the postseason. The more I followed the Royals, learning the stories of the players and the organization, the more joy I found in my life. Sure, I was disappointed with 100-loss seasons and when players left for other teams, but there was a concurrent hope and simple delight from once again listening to games on the radio, sitting in the stands on a summer's eve, or catching a few innings of a getaway-day game over a late lunch break.

Last summer, I had the opportunity to play catch with one of my childhood heroes—Royals' Hall-of-Fame second baseman, Mr. Frank White. By that time, it had been close to 20 years since I had thrown a baseball. In a matter of minutes, my dreams of playing for the Royals were as fresh as they had been when I was in high school. I went home and wrote the story as fast as I could, before I forgot any of the details. My friend Mike the Theologian read the story and thought it worthy of being published in *Immerse Journal*.

Later in the same summer, Rustin Dodd, a Royals' columnist for the KC Star, held a contest to see if anyone could write an anthem for the Royals. I scrapped my plans for the day, played around with some rhymes and rhythms, and submitted a scratch recording in just a few hours. A few weeks later, I was notified that I had, in fact, won the anthem contest.[1] My prize consisted of a t-shirt, a set of coasters, a lunchbox, and a stocking. I was secretly hoping for some autographs or a chance to hear the song in the stadium. I knew that if I tried to perform it live, I'd throw up.

For Christmas, Dad celebrated my Royals-related success—buying me the 1985 World Series Commemorative DVD set and season tickets to the 2011 games. The tickets arrived in the mail just a few weeks before Opening Day. I could hardly contain my excitement.

It took me a long time to realize that baseball in and of itself is one of the ways in which God speaks to me. Watching the Royals play this season led me on a journey of faith and reflection, one that softened my heart to hear God share His Story through this marvelous game.

---

[1] http://royalsblog.kansascity.com/?q=node/667

1

Opening Day

March 31, 2011
Royals' Record: 0-0
My Record: 0-0

"Nothing better
Than baseball. For kids.
Teaches them all the lessons."[2]
—Buck O'Neil

My dreams bleed Kansas City Royal blue.

As long as I can remember I have been enamored with the Royals. I went to my first game when I was four years old with Dad and Mom and ever since, my imagination has considered anything pertaining to the Royals sacred.

I love the new stadium, the powder blue uniforms, and the legacy of the I-70 World Series. I love the ballplayers—White,

---

[2] Joe Posnanski, *The Soul of Baseball: A Road Trip Through Buck O'Neil's America.* (New York: Harper Collins Publishers, 2007). All chapter quotes are from Buck O'Neil and are quoted from Posnanski's book.

Quisenberry, Brett, Jackson, Seitzer—who played with passion and intensity and a healthy dose of confidence. I love listening to Hall-of-Fame announcer Denny Matthews on radio broadcasts any summer night.

But right now it doesn't make much sense to love the Kansas City Royals. They have only had one winning season in the last decade, they just traded one of the best pitchers they've ever had, and they are picked to finish about 20 games below .500, which means they'll get another high draft pick.

During the off-season, I had the opportunity to meet a former major league ballplayer who loved the legacies of the teams that he used to play with, but hated what the game of baseball had become. He was frustrated with everyone from owners and managers to players who don't practice or play with an intense passion, loyalty, and love for the game.

I must confess that after the discussion with the former player, I was a little down-spirited. Here was a man who had the chance to live out my dreams, yet he had very little good to say about his experiences. I took a lesson from Buck O'Neil and looked for the silver lining in the situation. *Maybe he's just having a bad day. Maybe he's right and the game has changed, but that doesn't mean I can't still enjoy it. Maybe it's too early in the morning and he just needs a cup of coffee.*

As a Christmas gift, Dad and Mom bought me "season tickets" to the Kansas City Royals. By "season tickets," I mean I received two tickets to 20 different games. Translation: I would have the opportunity to watch about 25% of the games played at home this season.

At Christmas, Opening Day seemed like a million miles and a thousand years away, and every snowstorm, ice storm, and winter head cold pushed it back even further. Finally, *finally*, March arrived. I had a publishing deadline on April 1st, but determined to turn in my work on March 30th, so I would be free from any conceivable distractions.

Opening Day is that one sacred day when all teams are equal—when hope is eternal. It is the day when B-2 stealth bombers fly overhead during the pre-game ceremonies. Opening Day is to baseball what the first day of school is to kids: a chance for a fresh start, a chance to make new friends, a chance to dream big, to chase the impossible and think, *"This is the year!"*

Come Opening Day, I still had to finish a project at work. Only the assistance of a mocha from Doozen's Coffee enabled me to give it my full attention. Dad was driving up from Springfield and I was waiting for him to go to lunch and then the stadium.

Spring was in no hurry to greet the people of Kansas City. Opening Day was much of the same—cold and overcast with occasional light rain. Not even the weather could dampen my excitement. Dad greeted me at my office only 20 minutes from the stadium. We grabbed a quick bite to eat and arrived at the ballpark three hours early.

I officially counted eight people who made it into the stadium ahead of us. We were even there in time to watch the Royals take batting practice, which was a special treat. Standing by the left-field foul pole, Dad and I watched an exclusive Bob Costas interview with George Brett on the beautiful, enormous HD scoreboard, all the while hoping for the chance to grab a ball as a cheap and memorable souvenir. Royals' players were generous in tossing balls into the stands, but I couldn't beg or ask for one; I just wanted one thrown or hit my way. The Royals finished their warm-ups and the Los Angeles Angels of Anaheim took the field.

The majority of the Angels players gathered on the left field foul line to stretch and warm-up by playing catch. On a couple of occasions, Angels' batters came close to hitting one of their own teammates. I'd yell, "Heads up!" whenever it was close. As they wrapped up batting practice, a ball bounced particularly close to me. One of their trainers was running over to grab the ball when a line drive was hit right at him.

"Heads up, dude!" I shouted. The ball landed two feet behind him.

"Thanks, man," he said, as he tossed me the ball.

After batting practice, Dad and I walked the entire circle of the stadium, taking a moment to admire the bronzed statues of Dick Howser, Frank White, and George Brett in the centerfield pavilion. As we neared our seats, we ran into my friend Aaron, the concessions stands manager, who treated us to souvenir sodas and hot dogs. Dad and I settled into our seats next to two people who had to drive 180 miles to pick up their tickets from a FedEx station. The man had worked overnight and was visibly tired. He simply smiled and said, "It's awesome to be here on Opening Day."

We witnessed Royals' pitcher Luke Hochevar make his first Opening Day start. He made a couple of mistakes that landed a few hundred feet away over the fence, and some sloppy defense didn't help his cause. At the end of six innings, the Royals were down 4 – 0. Going into the bottom of the seventh, Dad, who still had to make the drive back to Springfield after the game, said, "If they don't tie it this inning, let's head out." The Royals had struggled all day against Angels starting pitcher Jered Weaver. With one out in the seventh, Weaver was pulled and Hisanori Takahashi came in to pitch—and the Royals' bats came alive. Jeff Francoeur hit a solo home run, and the Royals loaded the bases with two outs before Wilson Betemit struck out. We decided to stay for one more inning.

With two outs in the top of the eighth, Angels catcher Jeff Mathis doubled up the left-field line. Peter Bourjos followed with a solid single to right. Royals right-fielder Jeff Francoeur came up with guns blazing, throwing a rope to home on one bounce and nailing Mathis at the plate. The stadium went electric.

Mike Aviles led off the bottom of the eighth with a solo home-run, bringing the Royals to within two runs. The Royals continued to fight and scrap, getting runners on base and in scoring position for the remainder of the game. Hitters battled, fouling off pitch after pitch after pitch. One thing was for certain: this team played with heart and passion, with a chip on their shoulder and a desire to prove something. I thought to myself, *This team just might change the mind of that former player. There's something different about this year's team.*

Nearly frozen, we decided to go ahead and leave before the end of the game. Walking to our car, we took stock of the game. Dad and I had witnessed the major league debuts of Aaron Crow, Nate Adcock, and Tim Collins. The young KC bullpen looked sharp—even impressive—especially with Crow striking out three of the four batters he faced.

After the game, Dad took my family and me to dinner at a local Mexican restaurant. While we munched on chips and salsa, a mother and son approached me. "Are you Ethan?" she asked. "You coached Benjamin's first t-ball team six years ago. He's now playing in his fifth season, pitching, and absolutely loves the game. Baseball has been good for him." We talked a few more minutes and I showed him the ball I got from batting practice.

And then it struck me—baseball *is* good for us.

Baseball gets us out from behind cubicles and computer screens and concrete walls, where the cool wind blows and allergies tickle our noses. Baseball gives us the chance to meet new friends in nearby seats and to scream at the top of our lungs at a good play or the hopes of a game-changing at-bat. Baseball provides space for a father and son to spend an afternoon together, reminiscing of games and plays and seasons never recorded or seen by a large crowd. Getting caught up in a game helps us place the stresses and worries of life on hold—even if for just a couple of hours.

Baseball is also good for our souls, reminding us of some of the essential truths of life. When I was a kid, I'd entertain myself by turning everything into a baseball game—bouncing a ball against backyard steps or counting the number of consecutive green lights hit while running errands with Mom or Dad. But it wasn't the same as playing a *real* game.

It is impossible to play baseball alone. Baseball is a team effort, and success only comes when teammates rely on and trust in the gifts and abilities of everyone on the team. Some have gifts as specific as being a "lefty-specialist," while others are blessed as a complete five-tool player.[3] We did not choose our gifts any more than we chose our height and therefore have no room to brag about our abilities. We are to use our gifts for the good of the name on the front of the jersey, rather than the name on the back of it.

The lefty-specialist is called into the game at a critical juncture, with his team's success resting solely on his shoulders as he faces a left-handed hitter with runners in scoring position. He doesn't pitch in every game, and he doesn't pitch to every hitter. His gift is a refined craft and is best used in a specific situation. A kindergarten teacher does not teach high school students. A banker does not attempt to mend broken bones. A dentist does not cut hair, just as a hair-stylist does not fill a cavity. We are all on the same team, joining with brothers and sisters around the world. We use our gifts to help meet the needs of others and trust our "teammates" to do the same.

---

3 The traditional five-tool player has these gifts: Hitting for power, hitting for average, base-running skill and speed, defensive abilities, and a strong throwing arm.

A great cloud of witnesses—people who have played the game before them and people who are just learning to play the game—surrounds the gifted professional athletes on the field. The example set by those currently on the field teaches, inspires, and encourages all those with eyes to see and ears to hear.

Players move with every pitch, changing their defensive positioning with every hitter, fully invested in that moment. They recall the lessons of their dads and brothers and uncles and mothers, the guidance of their coaches and mentors, and strive for success with every plate appearance, every attempt on defense.

We are all lifelong learners. Wisdom comes when we learn through the successes and failures of others, not just through our own experiences. We have stories to live into from the previous generation and stories to pass on to the next generation. We live in the fullness of life right now, slowing down to be aware of the beauty of the moment, not worrying about tomorrow's unanswerable questions or chasing our dreams after we retire.

* * * * *

The Royals lost on Opening Day, much to the dismay of the 40,000 gathered fans. But one loss does not mean a failed season. In baseball, failure is inevitable. You will strike out. You will make an error. Your team will lose. The question is, do you allow yourself to be defined by your failures, or do you choose to hold on to hope and believe that next time will be different? We learn best from our failures, not from our successes. This team, I believe, will teach those who are willing to watch and listen many lessons on faith, perseverance, and hope.

Thanks be to God who has given us the good gift of baseball, where fields of play become fields of dreams for all ages—and fields of dreams become fields of faith for the child in each of us.

2

Baseball is Beautiful

April 1, 2011
Royals' Record: 0-1
My Record: 0-1

"*You see today, but I see history . . . I see little things that remind me. It's beautiful.*"
–Buck O'Neil

Baseball is a game filled with simple beauty. A low-scoring pitcher's duel. A well-timed double play. A game-winning walk-off home run. Each of these aspects in itself is beautiful, a delight to the seasoned baseball fan.

Along with my season tickets, Dad also gave me the commemorative edition of the 1985 World Series. Between Christmas and Opening Day, I watched all seven of the games in which the Royals played the St. Louis Cardinals. Back in 1985, Royals' stadium had an Astroturf field, general admission seats in the outfield, and no advertising on the outfield fence. With fountains that danced at the push of a button, the "clean-look" was a refreshing change to the visual experience that is now known as The K. My friend Brian the Rememberer also purchased the 1985 World Series DVD set, and we'd talk almost every week about the differences in the stadium, the players, and even the game itself. We finally agreed that with or without all the changes in the stadium, The K is a glimpse of heaven.

I invited Kaleb to go to the game with me under one condition—he must cheer for the Royals. Kaleb is a Yankees fan. It is a miracle that we are even friends. The first Friday evening of the season was beautiful—clear, crisp, a taste of spring in the air. With fireworks illuminating Kauffman Stadium after every Friday night home game, we hoped to enjoy a good game and then delight our inner-pyromaniacs.

Jeff Francis was the starting pitcher for the Royals, a crafty southpaw who relies on location and timing more than power. His fastest pitch of the night was clocked at 88 mph, fast enough to power a time machine with a flex-capacitor, but not fast enough to blow major league hitters away. With one out in the top of the first inning, Angels' second-baseman Howie Kendrick hit a long home run to straightaway centerfield, and with that the Royals were down 1-0 in the blink of an eye.

That was it for the Angels. Francis battled for the first few innings until he settled into his groove. A couple of timely double plays and lots of ground ball outs kept the Angels from mounting much of a threat for the remainder of the game. Francis pitched seven complete innings for his first outing of the season—giving up five hits, one earned run, one walk, and striking out four. He left with the game tied at one.

I was a sophomore in high school the last time I played competitive baseball. Easily the smallest guy on the team, I simply couldn't throw the ball as hard as my teammates—which is not a good thing for a pitcher. Late in the season with the game tied, Coach brought me in to pitch. I struck out a couple of hitters and got the others to pop out or hit weak grounders. Six batters faced, six outs recorded. In those same two innings, my team scored a few runs, and we went on to win the game. I was, technically, the winning pitcher. It was the last time I pitched in a "real" game.

A well-pitched game is beautiful. Though many people love the high-scoring games with lots of hits and runs, a low-scoring game shows that the pitcher is actually *pitching*, not just throwing the ball really hard. The primary job of the pitcher is to disrupt the timing of the hitter, keeping him off-balance and guessing at the pitch to come. A true pitcher gets in the mind of a hitter, like when Randy Johnson threw a pitch over John Kruk's head in the 1993 All-Star Game. A true pitcher does not have to overpower every hitter with a triple digit fastball but locates the right pitch at the right time, trusting his defense to make the necessary plays behind him. When pitchers pitch to their strengths, success will follow.

A couple of years ago, Mike MacDougal was the closer for the Royals. He could hit triple digits with his fastball and also had a wonderful curveball/slider that would buckle the knees of the best hitters. The St. Louis Cardinals were in town, and the game was tight. With two outs in the ninth, Albert Pujols stepped up to the plate. It pains me to admit it, but Cardinal red vastly outnumbered Royal blue in the stadium that day. Everyone in the stadium rose to their feet for the ensuing showdown. With two strikes, MacDougal threw perhaps the best curveball in the history of baseball. Pujols' knees buckled and his back turned as if waiting for the pitch to hit him. When it crossed home plate, the umpire shouted strike three, and the Royals celebrated a victory over their I-70 rivals.

Pitching is an art. When it is done well, major league hitters don't stand a chance of hitting the ball hard. In order to appreciate the art of pitching, one needs to be educated—just like one needs to be educated to appreciate the art of DaVinci, Picasso, Monet, and Pollack, hanging on the walls of museums around the world. A pitcher is doing his job well when lots of ground balls and weak pop-ups are hit, when no one is walked, and when he can strike out a hitter looking at strike three. I have seen some amazing pitchers firsthand: Nolan Ryan and Randy Johnson; Zack Greinke, Andy Pettite, and Mariano Rivera; Charlie Leibrandt, Dan Quisenberry, Roger Clemens, and Pedro Martinez. To watch a pitcher perform his craft—painting strikes on the corners and playing with the minds of hitters—is to watch a modern-day artist at work.

On this first Friday of the season, both Jeff Francis and Dan Haren, the starting pitcher for the Angels, pitched beautifully. The Royals tied the game in the bottom of the fourth inning when Billy Butler and Kila Ka'aihue each got their first hit of the season. With one out, both men singled and advanced into scoring position on a passed ball. Jeff Francoeur grounded out, and Billy scored the tying run. The game was deadlocked at one run.

*****

The double play is momentum changing, defusing the offensive threat and energizing the defense. Successfully turning a double play requires skill and timing. It is a matter of being in the right place at the right time and is as graceful as any ballroom dance. The prototypical double play is a sharply hit ground ball to the shortstop, who tosses the ball to second base, leading the second baseman. The second baseman catches the ball, steps on the bag, and throws to first while jumping over the runner who is sliding into second—all in one fluid motion. I once helped turn a double play in high school but didn't jump high enough, and I still have a scar on my left knee from the spike of the runner sliding in. I'm pretty proud of that scar.

Two outs, one play. There are endless permutations of possible double plays, and each one is beautiful in its own right. There's the "strike-'em-out-throw-'em-out" double play, where the pitcher strikes out the hitter and the catcher guns down the runner attempting to steal. The "6-4-3" and the "4-6-3," with middle infielders cheating towards second base to get to the bag in time, exchanging the ball and redirecting its momentum in a flash. There's the fly-out to an outfielder, who then gets an assist as the runner tries to advance to the next base. I've even seen two men tagged out by the catcher at the plate in the same play.

The Royals turned three double plays in that Friday game, and Kaleb the Yankees fan and I celebrated every one. Kaleb even commented on one occasion, "A double play would be really nice right here." Sure enough, a ground ball to third baseman Mike Aviles started an around-the-horn double play, and the crowd loudly cheered in appreciation.

The double play is a unique part of baseball; there is nothing like it in any other sport. When two outs are recorded in one play, with only three outs in an inning, the offensive team suddenly finds itself down to its last chance. It would be similar to sacking the quarterback on second down, and because the sack is so cool, the refs immediately declare it fourth down. A double play is about being in the right place at the right time and successfully converting the opportunity into a reality; that's where the beauty comes in.

* * * * *

Our culture has an obsession with beauty, narrowly defined as a perfectly manicured lawn, an expensive luxury car, or a supermodel's physique. But beauty abounds in life, if we know where to look.

Too often, we employ a superficial system of personal preference to declare something beautiful. Our judgments are impaired by cultural heritage, personality, and what we ate for lunch. It is very difficult to declare anything beautiful with an upset stomach.

It is often quipped that "beauty is in the eye of the beholder," a statement that can be applied to art and sport alike. But beauty is also taught to the next generation. Many young girls believe that the Disney princesses are the perfect pictures of beauty, dressing up and dreaming of one day meeting them on the hallowed ground of Disney World.

It is beautiful when one person serves a stranger because the opportunity presented itself. It is beautiful when someone does the "right" thing, even if no one else is there to watch. It is beautiful to make a new friend, to call a time out from life's hectic pace, or to go on a leisurely bike ride with the family.

Our hearts are naturally drawn towards beauty. Beauty stirs our souls and calls forth a response, which is actually a form of worship. Beauty is a reflection of the hand of the Creator, and when we acknowledge the beautiful, we are joining the song of all creation that constantly sings to the Creator.

*****

In the bottom of the ninth inning, the game was still tied at one. Royals' first baseman Kila Ka'aihue, who led the team in home runs during spring training, stepped up to the plate. I leaned over to Kaleb the Yankees fan and said, "With one swing of the bat, the game could be over." No sooner had I said it than it was. A 390-foot home run blasted to right field. The stadium erupted.

"Fireworks!" we both screamed.

A walk-off home run in the bottom of the ninth inning secured a victory for the Royals. A mob of players greeted the hero at home plate; fans celebrated, high-fiving strangers and sharing in the thrill of the last-minute victory.

Baseball *is* beautiful.

3

Never Give Up

April 5, 2011
Royals' Record: 3-1
My Record: 1-1

"Sometimes you just need a little something that makes you believe."
—Buck O'Neil

My oldest daughter, Kaylea, joined me for my next game. She was as excited as I was to get to the stadium and cheer on the Royals. She carried her roster around with her, matching up the guys on the field and learning about their heights and weights, birthdays, hometowns, and jersey numbers.

We headed to our seats anticipating another thrilling evening at the ballpark. But after only thirteen pitches, the Royals were losing 4-0.

Four pitches—triple. One pitch—single. Six pitches—walk. Two pitches—homerun.

Four runs scored after the first four hitters—a horrible way to start a game. In years past, the Royals would have rolled over and played dead, allowing the other team to inflate the ERA of every pitcher who entered the game. The fifth batter also got on base with a single, which was immediately followed by a coaching visit to the mound.

Coaching visits are a mystery. I like to imagine what discussion is taking place in this private conference witnessed by a few thousand people. On this day, it could have gone like this: *Well, this game's over. Just try to pitch as long as you can so we don't have to completely waste our bullpen in a blowout of a game. I thought you were going to do better than this. Man, you are such a disappointment.*

That is the typical human reaction. When someone is down and struggling, we like to beat them up a little more, kick them, and sprinkle in a few spoonfuls of guilt and shame to make sure they are completely humiliated. After a few days have passed and an opportunity for redemption comes, we quickly remind the unfortunate soul of their previous failure and offer little more encouragement than a mumbled, "Good luck."

But not today. Today's coaching visit probably went something like this: *Well, this game just got interesting. I bet they think they are going to walk all over you and send you to the showers early. But that's not going to happen. It's time to start over. Forget the runs; we'll get them back. This game's just started, and we're not going to give up. Somehow, we're going to win this one. You do your job like I know you can. Throw strikes. Trust your defense. This game is far from over. Don't give up.*

Three outs were recorded in the next seven pitches. Inning over.

In the bottom of the first inning, the Royals cut the deficit in half with Alex Gordon's two-run homer. The Royals prevented any more runs in the top of the second, and then tied the game in the bottom of the inning. The game was tied until the top of the sixth when the Royals committed an error and two more runs scored. The air in the stadium, however, was still filled with expectancy, and in the bottom of the eighth inning, Billy Butler hit his first home run of the season to tie the game at six. The game would head to extra innings.

* * * * *

There are very few speeches that stand the course of time, resounding throughout the decades, speaking to the deeper realities of life. From William Wilberforce's address to abolish slavery to Lincoln's Gettysburg address to Martin Luther King Jr.'s "I Have a Dream" address, saying the right words at the right time is a rare gift. Most of us prefer to insert our feet into our mouths instead.

On October 29, 1941, World War II had, for all practical purposes, just started. This war would become the deadliest conflict in human history, with some 40 to 70 million people dying. The war lasted six years, and all of the major powers in the world would be involved by war's end. Winston Churchill was visiting Harrow School, the school of his youth, to sing the traditional songs and to deliver a commencement speech. In one of his most famous speeches, Churchill said:

> "Never give in. Never give in. Never, never, never, never—in nothing, great or small, large or petty—never give in, except to convictions of honor and good sense. Never yield to force. Never yield to the apparently overwhelming might of the enemy."[4]

---
4   http://www.school-for-champions.com/speeches/churchill_never_give_in.htm; ac-

Little did Churchill know the weight and impact these words would have throughout history. Great speeches come in times of great need. Words are spoken to change perceptions and to foster courage and perseverance. Words have deep power to speak life and hope or condemnation and disgrace.

It is doubtful that anything uttered on the pitcher's mound between the manager and the battery would ever change the course of history. Still, whatever was spoken to Luke Hochevar in the first inning changed him, and from that moment he pitched near lights-out for the next four innings.

* * * * *

I am an indie musician. I play guitar, write songs, and sing. A couple of years ago I was in the recording studio working with Keith Kaster. Keith is a producer and engineer seasoned beyond his years. He loves to listen to a new song and then sing other songs that share the same rhythm and progression. He knows how music can speak to the depths of a soul and can arrange and mix songs so that their messages are felt, not just heard. Working with Keith, I quickly learned one of his mantras: "Persistence is the only talent." Recording music takes time, patience, and the willingness to dig in and sing again and again and again. It is easy to think, "I must not be good" or to say, "Good enough." Persistence means pushing through the struggle to that raw place within each of us to discover the genius. Unfortunately, too many of us quit before the going even starts to get tough.

Life is hard. Faith is hard. Paul once wrote to his friends, "Don't give up or get tired of doing what's good, what's right.

---

cessed April 18, 2011

When the time is full, we will harvest a bountiful crop, *if we don't give up or quit.*"[5]

God never gives up on us.

We give up on ourselves.

Many of us want some kind of cosmic pep talk—a divine visit with words to encourage us in the midst of our struggles and trials. We look for burning bushes and talking donkeys and ask for signs of all kinds. Maybe, in these days, as image-bearers of God continually being made new, we must be willing to recognize when others around us need words of encouragement. We know that God, when He walked among us, said, "I'll never leave you," and "All things are possible." And having once inhabited flesh and blood, He still uses those who are flesh and blood to deliver His messages of hope, life, and perseverance today.

* * * * *

When the Royals found themselves down 4-0, Kaylea turned to me with an expression of concern. "Dad, are they going to lose? Dad, this isn't good. What do we do now, Dad?"

I looked at her and smiled, "Kaylea, we cheer and clap and scream and encourage them as best as we can. They may not know us by name, but they will know we're pulling for them."

The next day was a school day, so we left the game in the top of the seventh inning. We continued to listen to Hall-of-Fame announcer Denny Matthews on the drive home and were pulling into our neighborhood when Butler hit the home run to tie the game. Completely exhausted and crawling into bed, Kaylea told me to wake her up and let her know when the Royals won.

It took twelve innings for the boys in blue to pull out a victory,

---

5 Galatians 6.9, mostly *The Message*, with some NIV, and emphasis mine.

but they did just that, winning 7-6.

I went into Kaylea's bedroom to share the news with her an hour later. She was snoring. I whispered in her ear of the victory, but she didn't remember come morning. She greeted me at the breakfast table and asked, "So? How did they do?" When I told her of the victory, she flashed her million-dollar smile and said, "I knew they'd never give up! I just knew it."

4

The View from My Seat

April 19, 2011
Royals' Record: 10-6
My Record: 2-1

> *"Funny,*
> *You look back,*
> *Didn't make no sense.*
> *Racism.*
> *No sense*
> *What people do to each other*
> *'Cause of something dark*
> *In their hearts."*
> —Buck O'Neil

How do you eat sunflower seeds?

I have one friend who eats her sunflower seeds one at a time. She holds the shell and gently cracks it open with her front teeth. Then, she eats the seed and tosses the shell on the ground, never tasting the salty goodness.

I have another friend who loves the flavor of sunflower seeds. He grabs a handful of seeds and funnels the whole thing into his mouth. He then chews the seeds like a large wad of gum. The seeds and shells crunch together into a flavorful mess. After all the flavor is gone, he spits out the whole disgusting gob, similar to a lump of chew, into a cup or a relatively out-of-the-way place in the grass.

Another friend of mine uses a combination of the above. He eats a couple seeds at a time, chews the mess together, *and then swallows the entire wad, shell and all.* Every now and then, he'll cough and tear up, saying something about a shell going down the wrong way.

With the arrival of flavored sunflower seeds, I've seen kids at the stadium lick all the salty, flavorful goodness off the shell, never to crack it open and eat the seed it protects. This reminds me of my friend who likes to lick all the cheese off of Doritos Nacho Cheese Chips before eating them.

I learned to eat sunflower seeds in the dugout. Placing a handful in my mouth, I store the salty gob in my cheek. I crack open one shell at a time, eat the seed, and then spit the shell out in front of me. It doesn't take long before a pile of shells starts to develop. On some days, those of us learning to eat seeds in the dugout would have contests to see who could spit the shell the furthest (un-cracked shells did not count). Other times, we'd have target practice with our shells. For me, sunflower seeds quickly became associated only with baseball. They are the perfect food for an anxious observer looking to dispel nervous energy.

My friend Eddie bought a large bag of ranch-flavored sunflower seeds on the way to the game. Before the night was over, we had left piles of shells all over Kauffman Stadium.

It was colder on this night of Holy Week than it was on Opening Day. I had on four layers of clothing, plus gloves and a thick jacket. Even through the layers, the wind was biting.

My seats for the season were up high, behind home plate. I knew how to watch a game from here. I surveyed the middle infielders as they positioned themselves for each hitter and pitch. I observed the graceful wind-up and delivery of the pitcher and had a pretty good idea about what was a strike and what wasn't. After each pitch, I glanced at the scoreboard to check the speed and compare it with the previous pitch. I knew where the pitch-count monitors were and could get a good read on a ball hit deep off the bat. I didn't bring a glove because I'm too high for a foul ball to reach me—and I was okay with that.

From these seats, we could see how far Alcides Escobar had to run to field the first ground ball of the game. Heading towards short right field, he made the catch, turned, and threw on the run. The ball beat the runner by a step for the first out, and the small crowd cheered loudly. Multiple replays lit up on the big screen.

On this particular night, no one was seated higher in the stadium than my friend Eddie and me. We cheered and ate seeds for the first three innings and then decided to change seats. With a wind-chill near the freezing line, only about a fourth of the stadium, which holds close to 40,000 spectators, was full.

If I were the owner of a baseball team, I would place workers in the stadium with a number of passes. After the third inning, if the crowd was particularly sparse, workers would be asked to distribute passes to people throughout the stadium for a free "seat-upgrade." The people could then choose to accept or decline the offer, realizing that they would be permitted to sit in designated sections on the field level. (They wouldn't be allowed to upgrade to the "all-you-can-eat-seats" or the dugout suites—that would just be crazy).

Our first choice of "new" seats was poor. We headed to the left-field foul pole. We were the only two people seated in the entire section. After one pitch, an usher asked to see our tickets. We graciously told him that we had tickets, but they were not for these seats. He smiled and said, "I'll have to ask you to move." Eddie and I laughed and politely obeyed. We started walking around the stadium, when four young men seated in the left field seats shouted, "Hey, you guys stayed there the longest so far, good job!" They encouraged us with high fives.

We decided to walk to the Party Porch, where the standing-room-only seats are, and watch the game from right-center field. I'd never watched a game from right-center field before. We were almost directly under the giant screen where I usually obtain all my in-game information; but the angle was too steep to easily read it. There are mini-scoreboards around the stadium that also display pitch speed information, as well as balls and strikes, but the game looked completely different from here. One guy close to us harassed the centerfielder for the opposing team the entire game. In the top half of the innings, after the Royals outfielders had warmed up, the people in the Party Porch would scream for the outfielders to toss a ball in their direction. Jeff Francoeur and Melky Cabrera obliged the fans, each flinging a ball into the stands. The outfield looked enormous and the grass was perfectly manicured, a close resemblance to my dandelion-covered front lawn. It was easy to see the location of pitches, even though home plate seemed a long way away. A couple of batters hit the ball in our direction, and it was amazing how fast it traveled.

Out on the Party Porch, there are lots of high fives with the people next to you, and lots of people dance and sing in hopes of getting on the big screen. Eddie and I never made it on the big screen, though we did leave some sunflower shells on the warning track.

In the top of the seventh inning, the Royals were leading 5-2. Cleveland's Lou Marson was on second base with two outs, and Michael Brantley was hitting. Bruce Chen, who had pitched a beautiful game thus far, was nearing the end of his night. Brantley lined the 1-1 pitch to left field, and Marson attempted to score. Marson was on third base as Alex Gordon scooped up the ball. The perspective from the Party Porch made it difficult to tell if Alex had a chance to throw him out. Alex rifled the ball on a line, arriving at the plate on one hop. Brayan Pena had the plate blocked and Marson was tagged out. Screaming and high fives were abundant at the Party Porch.

In the top of the eighth inning, I suggested we move once again. We decided to go for broke and walked up the first base line. We arrived at section 140, almost even with first base. It was late in the game, and there were still plenty of seats open. Eddie led the way as we hopped a row and tried our best to blend into the crowd around us. The guys to our left said the seats were open and welcomed us into "their territory."

From here, the players seemed huge. Kila Kaʻaihue and Wilson Betemit looked larger than the 6'4" and 6'2" listed in the program. Even through the wind we could hear the ball pop in the catcher's mitt. From here, I could see that the strike zone disappeared when Royals' closer Joakim Soria came in to pitch in the ninth. From here, I could see the odd angle and hop that the ball took as Kaʻaihue stretched for Betemit's throw. From here, I felt like I was part of the game.

In the top of the ninth, with two outs, bases loaded, and the Royals clinging to a one-run lead, clean-up hitter Carlos Santana stepped up to the plate. Soria completed the save with a three-pitch strike out—the Royals won. More high fives and some fireworks were followed by our quick dash to the car to turn on the heater.

On this night, Eddie and I enjoyed a game from multiple perspectives. Each perspective was unique and different, contributing to the enjoyment of the spectator. From up high, we could see everything that happened. From the Party Porch, we got a sense of what it would be like to roam and patrol the outfield. From first base, we could see the details of the players and hear the sounds of the field.

There are approximately seven billion people on the planet. That means that there are approximately seven billion different perspectives on life. Our perspectives are influenced by our cultures, our personalities, our ethnicities, and our preferences. As humans, we tend to label perspectives in order to better understand or control others: Liberal. Conservative. Rich. Poor. Red. Brown. Yellow. Black. White. Insider. Outsider. Creative. Analytical.

There is something to be learned from each perspective. Pain and injustice result when only one perspective is seen as "right." When we whole-heartedly support a biased perspective, genocides occur, the poor die of starvation and thirst, and young girls are trafficked around the world.

Humility is born when we acknowledge our biases and the limitations of our perspectives. I will always see the world as a white male. I have always been rich compared to the majority of the world. I have never been persecuted for my religious beliefs or had to walk miles to obtain drinking water or wondered from where my next meal was coming.

An important part of life is learning to see things from different perspectives rather than simply judging those who don't agree. The grade-school fight starts with, "My dad is better than your dad." International conflict starts with, "My country is better than your country."

Many missionaries who travel to foreign countries are more concerned about correcting cultural practices than learning the ways of the people. Politicians and priests alike preach a party-line propaganda that discourages dialogue and creative exploration.

I am a person of faith. I believe that we are supposed to learn to cooperate with each other instead of comparing ourselves to one another. I believe that each person on this planet is unique and different—a Masterpiece. The hues of melanin add beauty and the myriad of philosophies and perspectives make me consider and evaluate what I most deeply believe. Faith is supposed to encourage me to courageously explore all of life, not to fear the unknown. Faith is supposed to teach me to trust that God is with me wherever I go, not to rely on sight alone. This means that there are times when the perspectives and schemas I've developed to process life must be completely torn down and rebuilt when new and challenging viewpoints are presented.

It is good to change seats every now and then, to learn to watch the game from a completely different angle. I'm not saying you have to root for the other team, just be willing to continue to explore, to ask questions, to know that there is more to learn than can be learned, and to be okay with a little mystery in life.

After all, there is not a bad seat in the stadium.

And there is no wrong way to eat sunflower seeds.

5

Play Ball

April 29, 2011
Royals' Record: 12-13
My Record: 3-1

"You've gotta be alive out there! You've gotta play the game with joy!
Be alive!"
—Buck O'Neil

"Say it with me, Royals fans. Let's 'Play ball!'"

The stadium announcer exclaims it every game, right before the Royals take the field. Those two words are key to the start of a ballgame. When it was my turn to pitch growing up, I remember the umpire shouting, "Play ball!" and pointing at me to start pitching. Those words mean it's time to get serious about having fun.

* * * * *

My youngest daughter, Sophie, accompanied me to tonight's game. She had been counting down the days for the last two weeks until it was her turn to go to The K. To wake her up this morning, all I had to do was whisper, "Tonight, we're going to the Royals game." She sat up and picked out her Royals clothes, and immediately the questions started.

"Will you have to pick me up at school to take me to the game?"
"Will I have time to pack a backpack when I get home?"
"Can I bring Charlie (the stuffed animal) to the game?"
"Will we see fireworks tonight?"
"What will we eat?"
"Will we get to play?"

She got off the bus in mid-afternoon, ready and raring to go. The game started at 7:10; we arrived as the gates opened at 5:40. Immediately, we were greeted by a member of the K-Crew—the Royals' cheerleading troupe. The K-Crew walks around the stadium, conducting contests in-between innings and engaging younger fans during the game. Ebonee gave Sophie some tattoos and autographed a poster of all the K-Crew members for her. It was an immediate treasure. Sophie diligently looked for cheerleaders for the remainder of the night, hoping to procure more autographs.

We headed down to the left-field foul pole and watched the Minnesota Twins take batting practice. The wind howled out towards left field at a consistent 30 miles per hour. Sophie saw a few home runs and waved at a few players, all the while making certain her cowgirl hat from Papa didn't blow away. She informed me that real cowgirls tip their hats as a sign of respect and greeting to others. She tipped her hat towards the Minnesota players, and we walked to the Outfield Experience.

The Outfield Experience is a phenomenal part of The K. Younger kids can take batting practice in the Little K, and older kids can hit from pitching machines. Kids of all ages can be timed in a run to first base, ride a carousel, play putt-putt, climb on a jungle gym, dance in splash fountains, get their pitches clocked, and cool off in a video game lounge.

Sophie started out at the Little K, where she took five swings, got a couple of good hits, and ran the bases for a home run. We then rode the carousel together. She tipped her hat from high atop her horse; I tried desperately not to puke. After the carousel ride, we headed to putt-putt. In the five holes on the course, she almost made *three* holes in one. Finally, after golf, we visited the Frank White statue and gave him a high five on our way to grab a bite to eat. Sophie tipped her hat at the bronzed Mr. White as we left.

This particular Friday night was Buck Night. Sodas, hot dogs, and peanuts were all a dollar apiece. Buying a couple of hot dogs and Dr Peppers, we joined a few other Royals fans at the nearby picnic tables. A local magician entertained us while we ate.

When we finished eating, we were on the completely opposite side of the stadium from our seats. We decided to walk via the scenic route. Even though the air was cool, we stood for a moment taking in the view from the Party Porch and getting sprayed by the fountains in right field. We strolled to the foot of the enormous scoreboard and dreamed of what movies we'd like to watch on it. We walked by the Royals' bullpen to watch pitcher Bruce Chen complete his warm-up throws. Sophie and I were cheering him on when he looked up at us. Chen waved; Sophie tipped her hat. With less than ten minutes until first pitch, we headed to our seats.

For six innings, Sophie and I played ball *with* the Kansas City Royals. We clapped to the rhythms of various recording artists, danced in between innings, and cheered at the top of our lungs. Sophie taught me that the volume of our cheers helped the players to do their very best. We joined with 31,000 other fans in singing "Happy Birthday" to Veatrice Henson, who was celebrating her 100th birthday. To this day, I've never heard 30,000-plus people sing such a soul-stirring rendition of "Happy Birthday." We also sang, "I've Got Friends in Low Places" with the giant Garth Brooks on the scoreboard. Sophie didn't know the words, so she danced the song.

Seated two rows in front of us were a grandpa and a four-year old boy. From the moment we sat down, the boy couldn't take his eyes off of Sophie. In the top of the second inning, Sophie leaned over and whispered, "Dad, that boy keeps waving at me. I think he wants me to be his friend. Will you go meet him with me?" We climbed down over the seats together and introduced ourselves. The boy was enamored by Sophie's smile and hat. She sat down next to him and shared her pencil, and they drew pictures together.

In the top of the third inning, the grandpa offered to buy us drinks. He and the boy left, returning two innings later with a Coke and peanuts for Sophie. Sophie had never eaten peanuts in the shell. I taught her how to crack the shell open, and she and the boy entertained themselves for another inning playing peanut games with the wind. The grandpa introduced himself as "Peanut," saying that was the nickname he had had since his childhood.

Peanut and I continued to cheer on the Royals, sharing stories and experiences at The K. When I looked up, it was already 9:00, well past Sophie's bedtime. I knew that she wouldn't want to leave, so I planned a trip by Krispy Kreme donuts to help bribe her out of the stadium. We said good-bye to Peanut and his grandson, Sophie tipping her hat as we walked out onto the concourse.

On the way out of the stadium, we saw another woman leaving, walking on crutches. It was apparent (to me) that the woman had cerebral palsy, and the crutches were a part of her way of life. Sophie kept looking at the woman, and I was afraid that she would be offended by Sophie's stares. Sophie motioned for me to lean down, then whispered in my ear, "Dad, is she one of the Royals' cheerleaders? She looks like one to me." It was the most beautiful question of the night.

I walked over to the young woman and got her attention. "Excuse me, ma'am, but my daughter wants to know if you are one of the Royals' cheerleaders. She thinks you look just like them and would like your autograph."

The lady smiled and said, "Oh no, I'm not a cheerleader, just a season-ticket holder. Thanks for asking and have a wonderful night."

Sophie tipped her hat, and I picked her up and carried her to the car.

* * * * *

At some point, the vast majority of us forget how to play. When we really play, we aren't obsessed with keeping score or statistics, we just don't want the fun to stop. When we really play, we don't over-think or recite mental mantras to help us do our best; we immerse ourselves in life and feel the moment to the fullest. When we really play, we easily lose track of "normal" time. There is something sacred about playing that is lost when we attach numbers and dollars and careers to it.

A friend of mine is the executive director at the Christian Activity Center in East St. Louis, Illinois.[6] He is constantly telling potential donors of the important physical, emotional, and spiritual benefits of playing. Playing increases and improves circulation in the body and stimulates the brain. Children who play at least thirty minutes a day make better grades and have better self-esteem than

---
6   www.cacesl.org

those who are couch potatoes. It is essential to our humanity that we play. When we forget how to play, we quit reflecting part of the image in which we were created.

Unfortunately, we usually take play way too seriously. In order to "play," we have to have the right equipment and the right clothes and the right shoes. In order to "play," we have to be with the right people and on the right team to guarantee a victory so that we will have the most fun "playing." We take lessons so professionals can tell us how we can "play" just like they did, instead of forging our own path from the dirt.[7]

Tonight at Kauffman Stadium, Sophie and I played. When you play, new friends are made and snacks are enjoyed and someone always breaks out in a song and sometimes 30,000 people sing along. When you play, you are always making noises and moving around, and you must always keep an eye on the lookout for cheerleaders and others to invite to play along.

I think when Jesus said, "I have come that you might have life and have it to the full," he was actually saying, "Hey friend, do you want to come play with me?"

May we all remember that we are never too old to play—especially with Jesus.

* * * * *

In the middle of all of this playing was a Royals game. When we left, the Royals were losing 3-1. They scored a run in the bottom of the seventh and took the lead on a bizarre sacrifice fly to the shortstop, thanks to the amazing speed of Jarrod Dyson. Shortly after Sophie started snoozing, Joakim Soria earned another save

---

7   Golfer Ben Hogan is said to have beat his swing out of the dirt, and only by hitting tens of thousands of balls was he able to make a living doing what he was so passionate about.

as the Royals took the first game in this series against the Twins.[8]

*****

Sunday, May 1, 2011

Today was May Day. I don't know how to celebrate May Day, but seeing as it was a Sunday, I went to church, played bass in the worship band, and spent time sharing life with the teens who came to hear stories of Jesus and really play four square. Jamie, Kaylea, and Sophie arrived after the early service finished, and Sophie told me that I needed to look on the door handle to my bedroom when I got home.

Today was also the busiest day of my life. After two morning worship services, there was a lunch at church, followed by Kaylea's piano recital, then a baby shower for a friend, a birthday party for one of Sophie's friends, and the annual dinner celebrating our high school graduates. I returned home at 8:40 p.m., completely physically and mentally exhausted.

Just before bed, I remembered Sophie's words from this morning. I looked on the handle and saw a small craft. Sophie is always creating things with paper, glue, scissors, and whatever supplies she can find. She once told me, "Dad, my heart is sad when I don't have a craft to make." I can completely relate—I feel the same way on Royals' off-days and after I finish reading a book. This craft was a May Day gift—a construction-paper bouquet of flowers. On it, she had written in her very tiny but legible script:

---

[8] The Royals later went on to sweep the Twins in the three game series, the first time they have done so since 1994.

Der Dad,
Thainck you for taking me to the Royals on Friday.
I had a grat tim whith you.
    Love,
    Sophie

6

Civil Disagreements

May 3, 2011
Royals' Record: 15-13
My Record: 4-1

> *"It makes no sense,*
> *Hate.*
> *It's just fear.*
> *All it is.*
> *Fear something different.*
> *Something's*
> *Gonna get taken from you,*
> *Stolen from you,*
> *Find yourself lost."*
> —Buck O'Neil

According to MLB official rules, the strike zone "is that area over home plate the upper limit of which is the horizontal line at the midpoint between the top of the shoulders and the top of the uniform pants, and the lower level is a line at the hollow beneath the kneecap."[9] Should the pitcher throw the ball through the strike zone, it can be called a strike whether it touches the outermost boundary of the zone or is thrown right down the middle. Any pitch that does not pass through the strike zone and at which the batter does not swing is called a ball.

Theoretically speaking, that is. In reality, nothing is a strike until the umpire calls it a strike.

* * * * *

On the way to The K, I stopped with my family to look at a house that we were considering purchasing. For me, just thinking about moving is stressful, not to mention all the extra parameters my wife and I were placing on the decision. Our biggest factor concerned our girls. We loved the school the girls were attending and wanted to keep them in that school district. Unfortunately, this left us a very small community from which to find a house that would meet our limited budget.

About a year ago, I resigned from one of my jobs to create space for writing. My only guaranteed income was that of a part-time youth minister. Immediately, I was contacted about a contracted writing position and started finding outlets for some of my freelance work. When I called the mortgage loan representative, however, I learned that I had not been self-employed long enough as a writer to count any of that income towards our loan. All this really did was raise the amount of money we needed for our down payment, which wasn't that big of a deal. However, a couple of the projects I'd been working on had yet to sell, so the money we

---

9   *The Official Rules of Major League Baseball* (Chicago: Triumph Books, 2010) p. 35.

needed for a down payment wasn't really "mine," leaving me feeling horribly guilty and ridiculously stressed.

Jamie, the girls, and I walked through the *small* house and noticed that it would need significant repair work. Unfortunately for us, the genes necessary for craftsmanship and home repairs, alas, have somehow skipped me. Though I liked the house and could see its potential, I was overwhelmed by the amount of work necessary to help it become a home for my family. This fact, partnered with the financial stress, did not help my mood. I left quickly to go to the stadium.

While driving to The K, I called Jamie and vented my stress at her, telling her everything that was wrong with the property. (This was not my best decision.) I then drove to Chick-fil-A to self-medicate, promising Jake, the drive-through worker, that if the Royals made it into the playoffs this year, we could go to a game together. I arrived at The K in time to watch starting pitcher Jeff Francis warm up.

* * * * *

Mike the Theologian met me tonight at The K. Mike is a good friend and president of Youthfront, an organization that partners with youth ministers, churches, and other non-profit ministries to bring youth into a growing relationship with Jesus. Mike the Theologian and I have worked together on multiple projects. He has mentored me, encouraged me, and laughed with me. However, we have yet to play catch.

Two nights ago, the world was shocked to learn of the death of Osama bin Laden through a US military operation. I was watching *The Celebrity Apprentice* when President Obama made the announcement. Immediately, celebrations broke out across the country. I had had a busy day and was completely exhausted. I struggled to process the weight of the news. Yesterday, when I woke up, I continued to see pictures and hear stories of celebrations and revelry over the death of bin Laden. One friend exclaimed, "This is exactly what justice looks like." Another friend told me that "Hell was created especially for people like bin Laden." Nothing felt right to me about either of those statements. I knew the stories of Dietrich Bonhoeffer and how he helped plot an assassination attempt against Hitler. I could feel a connection between the death of bin Laden and the attempt against Hitler, but was too tired to think it through. So I sent Mike the Theologian an email asking for his guidance.

* * * * *

My friend Byron owns a bookstore in Dallastown, Pennsylvania, called Hearts & Minds Books. A few months ago, the Western evangelical Christian world was in an uproar because of a new book by Rob Bell. Though I haven't read the book, the risky subtitle offers a glimpse as to what stirred the controversy that followed—Love Wins: A Book About Heaven, Hell, and the Fate of Every Person Who Ever Lived. I have thoroughly enjoyed many of Rob Bell's books. He does a wonderful job of raising questions and challenging my selfish, biased assumptions. In this current book, Bell explores what the Scriptures say about Hell, and before the book was even released, Christians were calling him a "universalist" and a "heretic."

Byron engaged the reading segment of the evangelical culture by offering reviews and commentaries on Bell's book on his blog. However, before Byron offered his viewpoint, he first wrote about the need for civility, the value of appreciating diversity, and the importance of humility and respect for other believers. All too often, Christians argue with their emotions. We allow our feelings to get hurt and then purposefully strike back at the "other"—even when the "other" is on the same team.

In order to argue with civility, Christians must be willing to listen to one another, to appreciate the vast history of the "other's" perspective, and to have the honesty and humility to recognize that we can't possibly know all the answers. Jesus said that the world would come to know him, as we—his followers—love one another.

We are failing miserably.

Our foundational creed is this: Jesus Christ is Lord. If we can agree that Jesus was born, lived, was crucified, and was raised again on the third day, then we agree on what is essential. We are then given the freedom and the space to disagree over how many angels can dance on the head of a pin or what heaven looks like. It is imperative for us to learn to love each other, especially when we disagree.

* * * * *

The day after the announcement of bin Laden's death, Mike the Theologian posted this on his blog:

> Those who "celebrate" the death of Osama bin Laden, as if the USA had just won the World Cup, will bear some responsibility for the insane and violent counter-response that is sure to come. Why do we desire to provoke those who wish to harm us?
> As Christians, we cannot "celebrate" and as Americans we are foolish to "celebrate." This diminishes our humanity.[10]

---
10 http://king.typepad.com/mike_king/2011/05/celebration-is-an-inappropriate-response.

Immediately, people started posting responses and comments on Mike's site. The first few replies were supportive and resonated with the statement. Then people started using Scripture to defend their "shouts of joy when the wicked perish." He was accused of not being a US citizen and was, all in all, completely misunderstood.

Throughout the game, Mike and I visited about the death of bin Laden, the reactions of people around the world, and other similar theological questions. In the sixth inning, Mike received notice that Youthfront staff member Erik Leafblad had commented on the blog. Erik wrote:

> The lack of appreciation for nuance in this whole debate is astounding to me. Mike is not looking for empathy for OBL, nor should any be given in my judgment.
>
> None of what I have read from Christians deploring the kind of wanton (and drunken) celebration over this event serves as an apologetic for OBL. Yet I fear many who react to Mike's post, and others, read it as such.
>
> This is what ideology does, though. It blinds us to nuance. It robs us of sophistication. It pushes us to hear what another is not saying, all in an attempt to justify ourselves. If death is opposed to God's vision of life for this world (and what else could the resurrection mean?), then any death is grievous, even if necessary. Satisfaction and celebration are two different things. That is Mike's (and others') point.
>
> To be satisfied is permissible. To be celebratory and jubilant is to rejoice in war, to glory in the demise of one's enemy. War is hell. Sin is genius in its insidiousness. People are reveling in death.

---

html, accessed May 2011.

May God have mercy on us all.

This is civil disagreement.

Erik wrote with wisdom and heart and created space for those who didn't agree with him, while explaining his position. As for me, I finally found footing in the words of Martin Luther King, Jr.:
"Returning hate for hate multiplies hate, adding deeper darkness to a night already devoid of stars. Darkness cannot drive out darkness; only light can do that. Hate cannot drive out hate; only love can do that."[11]

* * * * *

Jeff Francis is a pitcher who relies on the reinforcement of the fullest definition of the strike zone. When umpires subtly squeeze the zone, his pitches get hit hard and often land on the other side of the fence. I arrived at the stadium early to sort through my thoughts about the house and bin Laden while watching Francis warm up in the bullpen. I saw him throwing strikes on the corners of the plate and was amazed by his accuracy. About halfway through his warm-ups, I was approached by a Baltimore Orioles fan. I tried to keep my distance.

Unfortunately for Jeff Francis, the umpire was not generous at calling strikes during the game. As the game proceeded, the strike zone got smaller and smaller. For the final three innings of the game, I started venting my pent-up stresses and frustrations at the umpire for not calling pitches strikes. "Come on, Blue!" I would shout in protest. (Everyone calls the umpire "Blue." I really don't know why.)

My friend Benson the Author always makes fun of people who

---

[11] Martin Luther King, Jr., *Strength to Love* (Minneapolis: Fortress Press, 1981) p. 53.

think they know the strike zone better than the umpire. "As if you've got a better view up here?" he questions. Many other Royals fans joined me in protest. Many of their comments, however, were not really appropriate to be written down.

There was a disagreement between what I perceived to be a strike and what the umpire called a strike. In the latter innings of a tied game, a walk often brings one team to victory. Every ball called was one pitch closer to a walk and the potential winning run for the Orioles, but my soul needed a victory tonight, and my vocal pleas for strikes were my prayers for healing, attempting to make sense of the world. The Royals pitchers continued battling through the ever-decreasing strike zone and getting Oriole hitters out. For the final four innings of the game, the Royals bullpen did not issue one walk.

Alex Gordon led off the top of the tenth inning with a walk, followed by a single by Billy Butler. Jeff Francoeur drove Alex in with a sacrifice fly to right field, and the Royals ended up winning 6-5.

* * * * *

The ballgame, the discussion, and the drive home gave me time to think about the small house. Yes, it needed a lot of work, but friends could help us with that. Yes, it would mean moving again, but following Jesus implies movement. I didn't know where the money would come from, I didn't know how the repairs would get done, and I didn't know whether the owner would accept our offer. I do know, however, that I was rude, not civil. I had hurt my wife's feelings and would need to offer apologies. I needed to slow down and listen, to see things from her perspective. I needed to remember that we are on the same team.

* * * * *

While I watched Francis warm up in the bullpen before the game, my thoughts stewing in confusion, I tried hard to avoid the Orioles' fan standing next to me. I wasn't in the mood to talk, and I wasn't in the mood to argue about whose team would win and whose team was better. He turned to me and said, "Isn't baseball such a great game? What a joy to be able to come out and watch it."

And I agreed with him wholeheartedly.

7

If At First You Succeed . . .

May 6, 2011
Royals' Record: 17-14
My Record: 5-1

"It isn't how long you live. It's how well you live."
—Buck O'Neil

Today was my sister's birthday, and all of Kansas City celebrated. More accurately, Kansas City celebrated the announcement that Eric Hosmer had been promoted to the major league team and was declared the starting first baseman. Hosmer was picked third in the first round of the 2008 MLB draft, and fans in Kansas City have not-so-patiently waited for his arrival. Tonight, the wait ended against the Oakland Athletics.

Starting pitcher Sean O'Sullivan struggled in the top of the first inning, walking the leadoff hitter and giving up a single to the next batter. With runners on first and third and nobody out, Oakland's Conor Jackson hit a fly ball to right field to Jeff Francoeur—one out.

If At First You Succeed . . .

Then, Godzilla stepped up to the plate.

Godzilla is Hideki Matsui. Matsui had a successful career in Japan and was "discovered" by the Yankees, where he played for seven years. In 2009, Matsui won the World Series with the Yankees and was voted the World Series MVP. In 2010, he played with the Los Angeles Angels and then signed with Oakland in the off-season. Matsui is always dangerous at the plate.

An uncomfortable feeling rumbled in the pit of my stomach as Matsui stepped up to bat. With two runners on and O'Sullivan still trying to find his groove, my imagination could see the ball landing on or over I-70. With the count 0-2, Matsui rocketed a groundball to Hosmer at first, who fielded it cleanly and turned a beautiful 3-6-3 double play, ending the threat in the top of the first inning. The stadium exploded.

* * * * *

I really needed a ballgame today. For the last year now, I've been writing and dreaming and hoping to find an agent, or a publisher, or anyone who would be willing to take a risk on a new author in this struggling economy. This afternoon, I received rejection notice number 55, which also happens to be Matsui's number. So far, I haven't been able to make any connections between the two.

One agent I recently spoke with told me that I didn't have a platform. His not-so-gentle advice was to stop writing and secure another source of income, then write for the joy of writing, instead of for the hopes of making a living. Out of frustration and a broken heart, I emailed Mike the Theologian and asked him about my "platform." He responded almost immediately:

Don't let anyone convince you that you can't do this. The greatest authors of all time had no platforms when they started writing. Their words *became* their platform. There is a difference between a writer and an author. A writer is a person who writes a book, article, or any literary piece, while an author is essentially the person who originates the idea, plot, or content of the work being written.

You are both a writer and an author. The kind of "platform" *Agent 007* is talking about requires a writer who can say something from their platform. Ethan, you will write in the future as you have done in the past. But your best work will be as an author, original content that comes out of your creative heart, mind, and soul. Unfortunately, this doesn't always get discovered quickly. Emily Dickinson was one of the greatest poets of all time. When she died, a mere seven of her poems had been published. After her death, 1700 were found and published. Ok, I don't say that to say you won't be read or thought about until after you're dead. I'm saying you have to write because you are passionate about it and about getting better—and if you do, you never know what might happen. One thing I know, as you write, God will smile.

I read that message *all the time*.

* * * * *

Kaylea is playing in her first season of girls' fast-pitch softball. The scheduling has already been crazy, trying to fit practices and games and tournaments into our already busy summer lifestyle.

She often requests my presence at her practices, which is a nice sentiment. When I'm able to attend a practice, I carry my glove and stand around and watch, hoping to get in on the action. It hasn't happened yet.

At practice, Kaylea is learning about all aspects of the game—covering bunts, which base to throw to in various situations, catching pop-ups, and taking swings. At practice on Monday, they focused on hitting. I've seen Kaylea hit before and know that she can pop the ball pretty well. However, during Monday's practice, she had an "O-for," with zero hits in more than thirty swings.

Tuesday, after school, Kaylea informed me that she was going over to her friend's house for more practice. She grabbed her glove and bat and headed out the door.

* * * * *

In the bottom of the second inning, Eric Hosmer got his first at-bat as a major leaguer. Hosmer received a standing ovation as he walked to the plate, and then, after working the count full, he received another ovation for walking to first base. I don't remember many ballplayers receiving that kind of applause for a walk. A couple of years ago, the Royals had a player who almost set a major league record for number of at-bats *without* earning a walk. I was at the game when he *finally* walked. He, too, received a standing ovation.

Hosmer's second at-bat was in the bottom of the fourth inning. Again, he patiently worked the count full and walked. He then successfully stole second base. Eruptions of applause circled the stadium.

The Royals were losing by one run when Hosmer got his third at-bat. With two outs and Jeff Francoeur in scoring position, the crowd rose to its feet anticipating Hosmer's first major-league RBI. He struck out on three pitches.

In the bottom of the ninth inning, Hosmer got one final at bat to start what has become this year's standard formula for victory: the last-at-bat-come-from-behind-walk-off-rally for the Royals. With plate discipline beyond his age, he again worked the count full. Instead of walking, however, he struck out looking. One of my friends was watching the game at home and texted me, "There's no way that was a strike."

The Royals ended up losing 3-2.

* * * * *

Two walks, two strikeouts, one stolen base, and errorless play in the field. Was Eric Hosmer successful in his major league debut?

We have a cultural obsession with success. We often determine success by our achievements and possessions: the size of our homes, the makes of our vehicles, and the bottom-line in our bank accounts.

Does it matter more which ladder you are climbing or who you are climbing with?

Does it matter which key you use if the door it opens just leads to another door?

Does failure necessarily lead you in the opposite direction of success?

Does success really define a person?

What if success was defined through relationships?

If humans were created to love and be loved, if humans were designed for relationship, then our definition for success needs to reflect our design.

As a parent, I want to give my children every opportunity for success in future years. However, for so many children and teens today, that is defined as being the next Olympic-athlete-rocket-scientist-soccer-all-star-Julliard-musician-*American-Idol*. We justify pushing kids into every available opportunity by saying that they are learning good values—teamwork, cooperation, discipline, authority, obeying rules, perseverance. I want to redefine success for my girls: to live a successful life is to grow in love for all people.

I have a friend who was talking to me about her days in high school. She explained, "I'd have volleyball practice after school and then drive 45 minutes to have another volleyball practice for another team. I was completely addicted to being ridiculously busy and stressed. I thought I was preparing myself for success. I just didn't know what success really was."

* * * * *

What is success when it comes to faith?
Is success being the pastor of a mega-church?
Is success getting your desired answers to prayer?
Is success knowing all the right answers?
Is success having your album or music on the radio or iTunes?
There was a guy named Jacob who struggled with relationships. He was the second-born of twins. His brother followed in the footsteps of his dad; Jacob was a momma's boy. He was also conniving and creative. When his father, Isaac, was on his deathbed, Jacob deceived him (with the help of his mom!) to receive Isaac's personal, paternal blessing. When his brother learned of this act of trickery, he vowed to murder Jacob after an appropriate time for mourning the loss of their father.

Then Jacob ran.

He fled to the land of his uncle, where he was married—twice—and worked with the livestock for years. He acquired wealth and servants and sheep and camels and donkeys. The time came to return to the land of his birth. Jacob's brother found out he was coming home and set out to meet him on the way. This was a terrifying thought to Jacob.

For the entire night before the encounter with his brother, Jacob wrestled with God. The wrestling match ended as the sun started to break over the horizon, and God blessed Jacob and changed his name to Israel, which means, "Struggles with God."

And this is the paradigm and foundation of our faith. Faith is the struggle. Success is the struggle. It isn't knowing all the answers or getting the desired results from time in prayer. Faith is wrestling and living in the reality of God's kingdom, which has already come in Christ but is yet to be fully realized on earth. To follow Jesus successfully is to embrace the reality of the struggle and to rest assured that he is always present with us.

* * * * *

Kaylea stepped up to the plate in her first game. I was sick to my stomach. It was 85 degrees outside, and I was freezing because I was so nervous for her. She didn't have any real concept of the strike zone and would swing at most any pitch. The pitch came and, sure enough, she swung, and *hit the ball.* She ended up with a double to the outfield and later scored on a friend's hit. She was elated.

She talked a million miles an hour in the car on the way home. In the middle of her stream-of-consciousness logorrhea, Kaylea rambled, "I was so nervous tonight. It felt so good to get a hit, even though I struck out later. But what made me happiest was knowing that you were there."

* * * * *

Eric Hosmer has a bright future ahead of him as the first baseman for the Kansas City Royals. He has succeeded at every level of baseball he has played.

However, what if his success as a ballplayer is not determined by his achievements on the field but by the contribution he makes to his community off the field?

What if, for every hit, home run, and RBI, area businesses donated services to reach out to friends in need around us?

What if Hosmer chooses a couple of non-profit agencies and makes consistent donations based on his game-day performances?

Eric Hosmer will definitely help the Royals win many games in the upcoming years. Hopefully, his influence will extend beyond the playing field and realm of baseball, encouraging Royals fans to lead lives of love for all people.

* * * * *

After her game, Kaylea's team shook hands with their opponents. Walking to the car, Kaylea passed by an "opponent" and complimented, "You did a good job tonight," flashing her million-dollar smile.

"*Success,*" I thought to myself.

8

It's All About the Numbers?

*May 20, 2011
Royals' Record: 21-22
My Record: 5-2*

*"Young scouts point their guns,
Write down the numbers.
Are they watching?
Really watching.
I wonder if they're looking for life.
Because that's the secret, man.
Miles per hour,
That don't mean nothing.
Does the fastball have life?
Does it move? Does it drive? Does it rise?
Bothers me. Too many scouts
Not watching for life.
Life passing them by."*
—Buck O'Neil

The St. Louis Cardinals are in town.

The guy sitting in front of me tonight wore the number 5. It did not say "Brett" above that number. It said "Pujols."

The first time I saw Albert Pujols hit, I was interviewing for the youth minister and worship leader position at Cornerstone Church. The church had tickets to a game against the Cardinals, and my wife and I were invited to go. When we arrived at the stadium, I ran into a family friend, who happened to know Pujols from the days when he played ball at Fort Osage. I had spent the last three years of my life in a seminary in Texas and was relatively ignorant of the current baseball world. I had been far too busy reading, reading, reading and writing, writing, writing.

In his first at-bat of that game, Pujols singled to centerfield. Then he singled to left field in his second at-bat. He doubled to right field a couple innings later. The church-interview game went into extra-innings, and the Royals won 3-2 on a home run by Mike Sweeney in the bottom of the 13th inning. I remember thinking, *"My first baseman is better than yours."*

I informed the guy sitting in front of me tonight that if he was to wear a shirt with the number 5, not only did it need to have a different name on it, but it also needed to be blue. He turned around and laughed. We continued to exchange playful banter throughout the game.

* * * * *

Chick-fil-A Jake predicted a sweep. I think he predicted a sweep because he was cleaning the facility, and sweeping is a part of cleaning. I would love to see the Royals sweep the Cardinals, but the numbers aren't good.

Brett the Artist met me at Chick-fil-A before the game so we could carpool. On the way to The K, we listened to the Royals' pre-game show and heard numerous statistics about the Cardinals. They said that St. Louis was leading the National League in offensive production, with the top team batting average of .283.

They continued to explain how effective St. Louis pitchers had been at shutting down opposing hitters, and how the club's rotation had the most shutouts in the National League, the highest winning percentage, the third-most innings per start, the fourth-best ERA, and the best ground ball to fly ball ratio.

They started talking about Albert Pujols and his tremendous success at The K. In 30 games and 138 at bats, Pujols was batting .383 with a .464 on-base percentage and 13 homers. He has only struck out eight times at the K.

When we got to the stadium, it was easy to see that of the 26,000 people in the stands, the ones cheering for the Royals were definitely in the minority. Cardinal red was—by far—the predominant color.

Tonight's starter, Jeff Francis, wore number 26. This is also the number that Kaylea wore this season. She became an immediate Francis fan since learning that she shared his number. At random times throughout the week, she would ask if Francis would be pitching that day. It always caught me off-guard. Unfortunately, in the paper, the number zero followed Francis' name. He had yet to win a game this season. Whenever Francis pitches, the Royals don't score runs. Not a good combination. In each of his last twelve outings, Francis received less than two runs of support. It's hard to win when your team doesn't score runs.

* * * * *

Numbers are funny things. According to the numbers, one man said that the world would end in 1988. I was in eighth grade, sitting in Mr. Freeman's Algebra class at the predicted time when all I knew would cease to be. Mr. Freeman noted that our time on this planet was nearing an end and advised us to spend our last minute in reflective silence. The only sound we heard was the clicking of the second hand on the black-and-white clock that hung on the back wall.

After what were surely several minutes, the minute came to an end. At the top of his lungs, Mr. Freeman declared, "I knew it! Math is heaven! Now, open your textbooks." We groaned in unison.

Numbers are a part of life. I recently met an accountant who loves her job. As I was rolling my eyes, she explained, "Numbers are unbelievable. They are awesome. Numbers help us catch glimpses of the Divine in the ordinary."

However, numbers can also ruin life. I grew up reading theology and philosophy every morning; it was called *Calvin and Hobbes*. For years, I woke up to Calvin, identifying with his orneriness, his curiosity, and his zest for life. In seventh grade, my two best friends Darren and Andy even nicknamed me "Spiff" after Calvin's daydreaming-outer-space-exploring-alien-conquering-superhero-alter-ego. Bill Watterson, the creative genius behind Calvin, poked fun at US Americans' addiction to numbers. Reducing a comic to mere words is an atrocity. However, I'd still like to retell one specific strip. Calvin was determined to become the world's best gum chewer.

Calvin: I need to get a heart rate monitor.
Hobbes: What for?
Calvin: To make sure I'm chewing at my aerobic threshold! Every day I want to see that I'm chewing more gum, faster, harder, and longer!
Hobbes: What's the point of attaching a number to everything you do?
Calvin: If your numbers go up, it means you're having more fun.
Hobbes: Science to the spirit's rescue once again.[12]

As a youth minister, one of the questions I hate the most is, "How many kids are you running?" Maybe it's an attack on my ego and pride or my lack of charisma and organizational skills— or perhaps my unwillingness to pay kids to come. If only eight kids are in my program, does that mean that I'm not a good youth minister? What does this number say about *anything?*

We attempt to measure the successes of churches with numbers. We count the number of people in attendance, the number of services held on a weekly basis, the amount of money in the budget, the size of the offering, even the square footage of the building. I have yet to see one attendance report that accounted for the presence of Father, Son, and Holy Spirit.

There are numbers throughout the Scriptures.

God dwindled Gideon's army of 32,000 down to 300, and then used them to conquer the Midianites.

A young boy offered up his lunch of five loaves of bread and two fish and ended up feeding a crowd of 5,000 men—not to mention women and children.

---

12 Bill Watterson, It's a Magical World (Kansas City: Universal Press Syndicate, 1996) p. 23.

Jesus said that wherever two or more are gathered in his name, he too is there.

Many people today are superstitious about the number 666 or have a fear of it known as *Hexakosioihexekontahexaphobia*. At the grocery store just a few weeks ago, the purchase of the person in front of me came to $6.66. She reached back and grabbed a pack of gum to add to her total.

This "bedeviled" number is an example of the practice of *gematria* and is found only in the book of Revelation. It is important to remember that John wrote the book of Revelation as a genre of literature that required interpretation. The practice of *gematria* uses "a numerical riddle in which words or names are coded as numbers."[13] Letters and numbers were interchangeable, making it possible to communicate in code. It is difficult to take a number and determine what name that number represents, as there are many possibilities. However, John's readers knew who 666 was—Emperor Nero Caesar.

The Greek spelling of Nero Caesar, transliterated into Hebrew, corresponds to a numeric value of 666. By the time of John's writing, Nero was dead. Domitian was the emperor. But Nero was the first emperor who persecuted the church of Jesus. John, symbolically, is warning churches of the emperor cult and of more persecutions to come.

My favorite biblical number is two, the number of coins the widow put in the offering. By our standards, it wasn't much. But by her standards, it was everything.

I don't think that God is impressed by our obsession with numbers. I know that they do not limit God.

---

13 Mitchell G. Reddish, *Smyth & Helwys Bible Commentary: Revelation* (Macon: Smyth & Helwys Publishing, 2001) pp. 261-2.

* * * * *

The numbers, however, didn't mean anything tonight.

The Cardinals spread out six hits over nine innings and didn't score a run. In the bottom of the seventh, the Royals scored three times—enough for the win.

And the best number of the night? One.

Jeff Francis got his first win of the season.

* * * * *

When I die, there will be two sets of numbers on my tombstone. They will look something like this:

August 16, 1974 – Month ##, 2###.

To borrow from a viral email, what is more important than the numbers is "living the dash."

Life cannot be measured by numbers, whether they be years or dollars or aerobic chewing threshold. Life can only be measured by love. And God's love is greater than any number imaginable.

9

The Big Picture

May 22, 2011
Royals' Record: 22-23
My Record: 6-2

"The greatest thing
In all my life
Is loving you."
—One of Buck O'Neil's favorite songs

When at all possible, I like to listen to the Royals' pre-game show on the radio. My favorite part is always the interview with manager Ned Yost. Today, Yost was answering a question about pinch-hitting for the young shortstop Alcides Escobar in the later innings of close games. Escobar's defense has been superb, displaying enormous range and a laser-like arm. However, his skills at the plate have yet to catch up to the major league level. In essence, Yost said that fans are mostly focused on winning today. His job as manager this year is to continue developing this young horde of ballplayers, preparing them to win for years to come. If he were to take Escobar out in close games, Yost would not be preparing him to be a success in the future. Yost said that it is imperative to manage with a view of the big picture.

In the bottom of the tenth inning, with the Royals down one run and a runner in scoring position, Alcides Escobar stepped up to the plate. Was it coincidence that just a few hours prior I had heard Yost talking about this very situation in the pre-game show? Immediately, I heard the voice of one of my friends asking me, "What if there is no such thing as coincidence?" I am pretty sure this is a quote from a movie, but for the life of me I cannot remember which one.

The Royals were not supposed to win this year. In the off-season, their farm system was ranked one of the best by numerous organizations, and it was said that the Royals should be contenders for years to come, starting in 2013. This year is a transition year, discovering where all the pieces fit, letting these young players find their footing in the big show. The fact that the Royals are actually winning is purely a bonus to the fans, a small taste of the good things to come.

At today's game, Robert Benson, the author, joined me. Benson is a wordsmith, a writer of sentences and stories and books. Several times throughout the year he leads prayer retreats for small groups and speaks at churches and conferences, doing book tours here and there. He is in Kansas City this week to lead such a retreat for a small group of men, and he flew in a day early to go to the Royals game with me.

I first met Benson the Author a year ago, when he came to town to speak at a church that was reading his then-newest book, *The Echo Within*. I had first contacted him after reading that same book. It was given to me from Byron the Bookstore Owner as a congratulatory gift, celebrating the publication of my first work.

Benson's book caught me completely by surprise.

For months, I had been trying to discern the whisper of God in my life, and his book helped me to better sort out my thoughts and act on my impressions. I wrote to Benson and told him that I thoroughly enjoyed his book. A few weeks later, he sent me a postcard with an invitation to call him at my convenience. He told me that he would be coming to Kansas City to speak at a church and invited me to have dinner with him. At dinner, I ate Chicken Spiedini and asked a lot of questions about writing. I listened very hard to his answers, scratching them down on a scrap piece of paper I found in my car after I dropped him off at his hotel.

I have emailed many follow-up questions throughout the past year and diligently tried to heed his advice as best as I could. Though I have continued to get published here and there, I have been unsuccessful in following his number one piece of advice—get an agent.

I was truly excited to go to the Royals game with Benson, knowing that he, too, is a fan of the game, and I still had a few more questions about this business of making "dark marks on a page."[14]

* * * * *

After winning their first game against the Cardinals 3-0, the Royals lost the second game in this iteration of the I-70 series by the same score. Today's game was the rubber match, and the stadium was definitely the Cardinals' second home. Again. Throughout the game, Benson questioned me numerous times about who the home team was and why there were so many people wearing Cardinal red. In our seats, fans of the red team surrounded us. Very

---

14 This is the title of Benson's latest book, where he writes about writing.

vocal fans of the red team.

The Cardinals jumped out to an early lead. Every time they scored, the very vocal fans of the red team would scream. Benson motioned for them to calm down and take a deep breath, fearful that their exuberant cheering might crush my fragile heart. At the halfway point in the game, the Royals were losing 7-1. Still, I knew that the Royals play well in the latter innings and had a feeling that it wasn't over yet.

There is a reason that a baseball game is nine innings long. It's the same reason that a game of golf is played over eighteen holes and a football game has four quarters and bowling has ten frames.

The Royals resurgence started in the bottom of the fifth inning, scoring a run when the Cardinals second baseman missed a pop-up. A few home runs later, the game was tied. I really, really wanted to gloat and shake my finger at the family seated behind us. I really, really wanted to say some rude and not-so-Jesus-like things to them. It was the good grace of God that they had left in the previous inning, preventing me from making a fool of myself, which is exactly what I would have done.

* * * * *

Yesterday was May 21, 2011. According to a radio preacher from California, the world was supposed to end yesterday. Jesus was supposed to come back and take some 200 million believers to heaven, leaving chaos on earth. I think this was the third or fourth time in my life that the world was supposed to end and didn't. This preacher has been described as a prophet and is supposed to be proclaiming the gospel of Jesus Christ. That means that when I try to tell others that I follow Jesus, they might think that I am like this preacher from California.

Not too long ago, there was a church on the other coast of this country that was burning the Koran. Because of their proclamations and actions, some US soldiers were killed in the Middle East. Some people might think that as a follower of Jesus, I also burn the Koran.

Both of these churches grabbed a very tiny portion of Scripture, closed their eyes, and held on tight. They manipulated the words that had been printed on thin pages. They did not see the big picture, namely, that God is still writing His Story. Instead of trusting God's Great Story that continues to be written by the Living Word, they twisted the written word. We, on the other hand, are to keep our hands and eyes open wide, living with great humility and even greater love.

* * * * *

In the Scriptures, the Greek word for "word" is *logos*. *Logos*, according to Greek philosophers, gave order to the universe and was the foundation of reason.[15] Philo, who interpreted the stories of the Hebrew Scriptures in the first century, understood *logos* as the intermediary between God and the rest of Creation. The personification of *logos* in Jesus changed everything.

I grew up in a Baptist church. Baptists take a certain pride for being known as a "people of the Book." They are also known for defending and defining the words of Scripture. With descriptions such as "perfect," "flawless," "inerrant," and "infallible," they use words to try and control *the* Word. I have seen Bibles cared for

---

15 Watson E. Mills, Editor, *Mercer Dictionary of the Bible* (Macon: Mercer University Press, 1997) p. 520.

like children, dressed up and imprinted with names—as if by paying more attention to the outside of the book, the inside can be better ignored.

Too many times, I have seen people forcing the Scriptures to say whatever they want them to say. I have witnessed debates about science and creation, the evils of Harry Potter, and why grape juice is closer to the wine that Jesus drank than real wine. One guy recently tried to convince me that the Bible predicts the destruction of the US economy through wars based on oil and the formation of a one-world government. He would only use the King James Version.

For Baptists, food is a necessary part of every church function. But no one dares to preach about the sin of gluttony while thousands starve to death on a daily basis. We wrestle with who can participate in taking the Lord's Supper (isn't His table open to anyone?), but not with who is called to give everything away. As Rich Mullins said in reference to the Scriptures, "I guess that's why God invented highlighters, so we can highlight the parts we like and ignore the rest."[16]

One day, Jesus was walking through town and healed a man who had been an invalid for 38 years. The day on which the healing took place happened to be a Sabbath. Immediately trouble ensued. Jesus and the man who was healed were both questioned by Jewish authorities. These authorities knew the Scriptures inside and out; most of them probably had the majority of what we know as the Old Testament memorized. In his defense, Jesus finally said, "You diligently study the Scriptures because you think that by them you possess eternal life. These are the Scriptures that testify about me, yet you refuse to come to me to have life."[17]

---

16 Shane Claiborne, *Irresistible Revolution: Living as an Ordinary Radical* (Grand Rapids: Zondervan, 2006).
17 John 5.39-40

We, too, have committed the sin of "bibliolatry," elevating the Scriptures above the Savior. We memorize bits and pieces, picking and choosing our favorite passages throughout the corpus. We obsess about reading the Bible from cover to cover, making sure that we spend a certain amount of time each day devoting ourselves to it when Jesus came preaching freedom from all religious traditions. Is it possible that we prefer the relative comfort of written words to the mystery and risk of following a risen Lord?

Jesus is the Living Word. We who are followers of Jesus do not live on bread alone, but on the Word that came from the Lord.[18] We understand that Jesus is the Way on this bizarre and incredible journey of life, and that He guides our feet and illuminates our path.[19] Jesus is the Word who came down from heaven and did not return empty, but completed all that God desired and purposed.[20] Jesus is the Word who continues to speak and hold all things together.[21] And Jesus is the Word who judges the thoughts and attitudes of our hearts, penetrating to the very essence of our being.[22]

* * * * *

The Royals pitchers had trouble with the strike zone today—they couldn't find it. All in all, they walked *thirteen* batters, including two with the bases loaded in the top of the tenth inning forcing in two runs. Alcides Escobar had an opportunity to tie the game with two outs in the bottom of the tenth inning and, to add insult to injury, struck out looking. This was just one game; the season is comprised of 162 games. Escobar is still learning, and I have a

---

18 Deuteronomy 8.3
19 Psalm 119.105
20 Isaiah 55.10-11
21 Colossians 1.17
22 Hebrews 4.12

feeling that good things are going to come from him.

Benson and I parted ways. I headed to my car, turned on the radio, and listened to the post-game show. In the seventh inning, Royals catcher Matt Treanor and manager Yost were ejected for arguing with the home plate umpire. Both were asked about what they said to merit the ejection. Yost responded that the umpire was a young umpire with a very tight and somewhat inconsistent strike zone. Yost also said that we have to remember that the umpire is just as human as the rest of us—a real person who has possibly the hardest job in baseball. All of a sudden, I saw the big picture.

The guys on the field are also fully human, amazing creations of God, whether they wear blue or red or black. The fact that they are able to make ridiculous sums of money playing a game is mostly a commentary on the screwed up priorities of our culture in this broken world. Off the field, the majority of them are just average guys who love their families and are trying to make a difference in their corners of the world.

Throughout the game, Benson and I talked about baseball and church and the end of the world. We talked about things that were beautiful and good, things that were painful and hard.

I have a friend who has told me that he doesn't believe in God. Sometimes he asks me questions about stuff he hears on the news. I knew I'd be seeing him in a couple of days, and I knew that when I did see him, he'd ask me about the prophet from California. I inquired of Benson what he thought I should say.

Benson replied, "Tell him the guy in California was—what's the word—full of baloney."

After a moment's pause, Benson continued, "There are three things to remember about the big picture. First, God is Love. Second, somehow, this God of Love walked around on this planet in the person of Jesus. Third, if you believe one and two, your life will never be the same."

And he took a sip of his beer and smiled.

10

Remembering

May 30, 2011
Royals' Record: 23-29
My Record: 6-3

"Memory is like baseball.
You might go oh-for-four today.
But you'll get three hits tomorrow.
Right? Good days and bad days.
You'll remember.
Those stories aren't gone.
They're just behind a few cobwebs."
—Buck O'Neil

Brian is a Rememberer. Every time I see Brian, he says, "Hey Ethan, do you remember—" and then he starts listing the names of various ballplayers from yesteryear. Since Brian and I comprise two-thirds of the percussion section in our church band—he plays the drums, I play the bass—we have ample time for remembering together. At one point or another, Brian and I have recalled almost all of the Royals greats: Bo Jackson and Bret Saberhagen, John Wathan and Willie Wilson, Hal McRae and Frank White and Amos Otis, Danny Jackson and Jim Eisenreich. We have also remembered other names such as Kirby Puckett, Kevin Mitchell, Cal Ripken, Billy Buckner, and Nolan Ryan. It's a fun exercise, recounting the players from the past, discussing specific plays and highlights of their careers. If our remembering is correct, it turns out that Brian and I were probably at a couple of the same games in decades past, long before either one of us knew the other.

Today was Memorial Day, a day set aside for remembering. Ironically, the origin of Memorial Day is forgotten, lost in history, and it is nigh impossible to determine where it was first recognized. However, on May 5, 1868, General John Logan of the Grand Army of the Republic made an official proclamation to honor those who had died in service to the nation by placing flowers on the graves of Union and Confederate soldiers at Arlington National Cemetery at the end of the month. Now, the last Monday in May is recognized as Memorial Day. Today, the very uniforms of the players reflected the patriotic spirit. The emblems on the hats of the Royals and the Angels were filled with the design of the American flag. Throughout the game, current Royals players gave tributes of thanks on the big screen for the veterans who once served or who currently serve in the military.

Before the game started, there was a brief video remembering the career of Royals' left-handed pitcher and announcer Paul Splittorff, who recently passed away due to complications from melanoma. Splittorff is the Royals' all-time leader in wins with 166, one more than Sandy Koufax. His voice and presence within the Royals' organization will be greatly missed.

Baseball is full of memories. The flags that wave in left field remind us of successful seasons of years past. Numbers are displayed throughout the stadium, reminding us of people who once wore the home team colors. Bronzed statues stand in the Outfield Experience, and pictures and stories dominate the Hall of Fame, allowing us to catch glimpses of the giants who once patrolled this outfield and ran these bases.

The game itself started off with a bang. The Angels played small ball in the top of the first to score, but the Royals quickly responded in their half of the inning. On the very first pitch, Alex Gordon uncorked a mighty swing, and the ball landed 420 feet away on the other side of the centerfield fence. Two hitters later, Eric Hosmer pulled one into the right field seats and, by inning's end, the Royals were leading 3-1.

In the middle of the game, Jamie and I joined a mom and a dad in the seats behind us in a game with their daughter. They were quizzing her on the retired numbers posted in left field: 5, 10, 20, and 42. We gave her creative hints ("See that bridge? It's named for the guy who wore number 5.") We told stories to help her remember the ballplayers those numbers represented. We even added random trivia associated with each of the numbers as well. Brian would have had a blast playing this game.

In my opinion, another number should be added to the wall in left field: 29—Royals' reliever Dan Quisenberry.[23]

Dan Quisenberry, simply known as the Quiz, was one of my pitching idols. Quiz was the submarine reliever, and, along with the number 29, he sported a thick red mustache. I doubt his fastball ever hit 90 mph, but he also once said, "I've always felt that

---

[23] Mike Sweeney was the latest Royal to wear number 29. During Spring Training this year, he signed a one-day contract with the Royals so he could retire with the team. I don't know if he wore the number because of Quiz or not. He wore the number well and I think Quiz would have been proud to share it with him.

when I throw it something wonderful is going to happen."[24]

Quiz made the most of the gifts he had, and his career was nothing short of amazing. Bill James, the modern-day baseball statistician guru, once said, "There has never been a pitcher who made fewer mistakes than Dan Quisenberry."[25]

In the 1,043 innings Quiz pitched, he

- Coaxed 130 batters to ground into double plays.
- Threw only *four wild pitches.*
- Gave up only 59 home runs. Of the 40 men who have saved 200 or more games, only Mariano Rivera has allowed fewer home runs per nine innings.
- Had 245 assists, which is 100 more than Hall of Famer Bruce Sutter had in his career.
- Walked just 162 men, but even this is deceiving because Quiz walked 70 of his batters intentionally. Quiz's one unintentional walk per 11 innings is, *by far*, the best walk ratio in the history of baseball.

Five times Quiz led the league in saves. Four times he finished in the top three in Cy Young balloting. His 2.76 ERA, compared to the pitchers' ERA of his time, is one of the best totals in baseball history. Every time I look out at those numbers in left field, I remember Quiz's legacy and think to myself that his number should be with them.

* * * * *

On this day of remembering, I remembered both of my grandfathers who served in World War II.

---
24 http://joeposnanski.blogspot.com/2010/09/ode-to-quiz.html; Joe Posnanski has petitioned for Quiz's election to the Hall, and these stats were located on his blog, accessed June 2011.
25 Ibid., accessed June 2011.

Grandpa Bryan, Dad's father, was a pilot. Two of his planes were shot down. He was an airborne spotter for the 44th Field Artillery, radioing enemy positions to the big guns on the ground. He rarely talked about his time in the service to Dad and my aunt, though he once commented that he flew over the hills where Julie Andrews sang in *The Sound of Music*. He said it was beautiful and reminded him of being home in Colorado.

He had a stroke when I was four years old and died when I was in second grade. I remember visiting him at his house, after the stroke had stolen his ability to make intelligible words. On multiple occasions over the course of that visit, he pointed and grunted, and I was able to correctly interpret his intentions.

Mom's dad flew in a plane as well. He flew on a B-17 from bases all over the United States, keeping Grandmon living out of a suitcase for more than three years. Decades later, we would play golf and work at his store together. We would sing at church and eat and have fun. He never once commented on his experiences in the service.

On this day of remembering, I wished I could hear them share their stories about the time they spent serving their country. I want to know their perspectives on war and our tendency to glorify what is a horribly normal part of life on this planet. I want to know the United States as they remember it, and hear their reflections on the Depression and living through the struggles of civil rights. *If only I knew then what I know now.*

More than 4,500 ballplayers changed their uniforms from baseball flannels to military colors during World War II.[26] Future Hall of Famers like Bob Feller, Hank Greenberg, Joe DiMaggio and Ted Williams lost vital playing time in the prime of their careers.[27]

---

26 http://www.baseballinwartime.com/, accessed July 2011.
27 Ibid. What is far less commonly known is that at least 130 minor league players lost

These players sacrificed their careers for their country. We don't hear about players doing that today. The United States was different back then.

* * * * *

I love the United States of America; I really do. I deeply appreciate our many freedoms and respect our civil and peaceful transitions of power. I love traveling, seeing the brilliant and amazing sights in this country, among my favorite being the mountains of Colorado. In my humble opinion, it is the best country in the history of the world.[28] But I am not an overly patriotic guy, and I am frequently misunderstood on this issue.

Tony Campolo is a preacher and risk-taking-truth-teller from Philadelphia whom I have met on a couple occasions. I first saw him when I was a student at the University of South Carolina, and he gave me a hug. I met him many years later when I was in seminary, and he gave me a kiss on the cheek and whispered a prayer in my ear. I guess Italians do that kind of thing regularly. Campolo once said, "People, I love this country. It is the best Babylon on the face of this earth, but it's still Babylon. This is not the kingdom of God and my ultimate allegiance belongs to Jesus—and so does yours." This is exactly how I feel about the United States.

One of my favorite verses in all of Scripture is a loose translation I did of Matthew 6.33: "Seek first God's Great Story and His Justice, and God will take care of everything else." In my experience, working within the church for more than a decade and partnering with numerous other churches, too many place too great a priority on fitting into the empire of the United States and end up

---
their lives while serving their country.
28 It needs to be noted—I'm not really a historian.

ignoring the importance and priority of God's kingdom.

If our desire is for the United States to truly be the best country in the world, then we should love our neighbors as ourselves. If we put love into action— feeding the hungry, providing clean water to the thirsty, helping to educate the children of the world—we won't have to worry so much about defending and securing ourselves from "them." Unfortunately, more often than not, churches lead the way in praying that God will bring His vengeance on the enemy and blow them to smithereens. The Way of Jesus, however, is peace through service, through love, and through compassion. There is a naïve part of me that still believes that love withheld is the root issue of all wars.

*****

On this day of remembering, we sang "God Bless America," which has become a standard at numerous sporting events after the 9/11 tragedies. However, especially in Major League Baseball, so many players aren't just from the United States. How do they feel asking God to bless this country instead of their homeland, whether it's the Dominican Republic or Mexico or wherever? What if we changed it to "God Bless All Motherlands?" Somehow, though our technology has enabled us to befriend people all around the world, and though we offer opportunities to talented people to come and play here, we refuse to acknowledge the other countries that make this game so great.

*****

Quiz was also a rememberer. After his pitching days were finished, he turned to poetry and wrote a book called *On Days Like This*. In a poem entitled, "A Career," he wrote:

> *It seems like yesterday*
> *it seems like never*
> *it lasted so long*
> *it went so fast*[29]

That's exactly what life feels like. And that's exactly why we all need to practice remembering. Intentional remembering takes those so-long, so-fast moments and freezes them, enabling us to glean their wisdom and truly learn from them. Remembering helps us trace the influences of generations prior, who served and sacrificed and taught us to love and live. Remembering reminds us that we are not self-made, self-sufficient, or infallible beings, but people who only live by sharing life, gifts, and resources with others.

The word "remember" occurs throughout the corpus of Scripture as an invitation to slow down and recall what truly matters. We are to remember the Sabbath or, in other words, realize that we aren't machines and that naps are holy events, too. We are to remember the works of God. David kept Goliath's sword and the early church circulated the letters of Paul and Peter and Matthew and John to help keep the stories of God's divine intervention in human history near the front of their minds. We are told that, thanks to the once-and-for-all sacrifice of Jesus, God no longer remembers our sins. (This, by itself, is good news that demands to be shared.) We are instructed to remember the poor, to remember our Creator, and to remember that we are made from dust.

---

[29] Dan Quisenberry, *On Days Like This* (Kansas City: Helicon Nine Editions, 1998) p. 38.

Remembering takes time and space. Sometimes we remember with friends and food, and sometimes we remember in that silent place between asleep and awake. It is imperative that we regularly take the necessary time to remember those who now join us in the great cloud of witnesses, for their stories are all part of God's Great Story.

* * * * *

As it turned out, while I was reminiscing on the days of the Quiz, we could have used him today. With winds gusting at nearly 40 mph, there were plenty of home runs. Unfortunately, after the first inning, they all belonged to the other team. Though the Royals led for the majority of the game, their all-star closer, Joakim Soria, struggled, and the Royals lost the game in the 9th, 10-8.

Immediately after the game, Soria approached manager Ned Yost and asked to be demoted from the position of Royals' closer. To accept that kind of responsibility and admit defeat is difficult, and it is a testament to Soria's courage and character. It reminded me that in baseball, as in the military and life in general, there is no place for showboating or selfishness. We do our part for the greater good of our team and our brothers and sisters around the world.

Even though I could never be one of those guys in the military firing guns at someone else, I can proudly remember the courage and character of the men and women who chose to honor their country with their lives, thanking them for living out their love. To take only one day a year to remember them is the least I can do.

11

Baseball Is for Friends

June 6, 2011
Royals' Record: 25-34
My Record: 6-4

"If Willie was up there (on the television)
People would stop making laws.
They would stop running.
They would stop arguing about
Little things
Or big things.
No Democrat or Republican,
No black or white,
No North or South.
Everyone would just stop,
Watch the TV,
Watch Willie Mays make that catch.
That's baseball, man."
—Buck O'Neil

I have never—no, not ever—listened to Rush Limbaugh on the radio. I have heard bits and pieces of his story, but I really know nothing about the man. After tonight's game, however, I think Rush and I could be friends.

* * * * *

At 4:00 in the afternoon, my friend Becca texted me, "Wanna go to a Royals' game?"
I replied, "When?"
"Tonight?"
Basically, Becca and her sister, Mary Kate, were bored and looking for something to do. Oddly enough, I had already planned to attend tonight's game with Kaylea. We had just returned from a weekend at the lake with friends from church, and going to a game sounded like the perfect way to start the week. At the lake, Kaylea spent a lot of time hanging out with Becca and Mary Kate. When you're ten years old, teenagers and twenty-somethings are the epitome of cool. They bought a couple of tickets using Stub Hub that were very close to my original seats. At 6:00, Kaylea and I picked them up, and we headed to The K.

* * * * *

My wife and I are trying to buy a new house. It has been a horrible, terrible, educational experience. For the last year, my family has shared a house with another family, learning to live in community. The experience in communal living has been beautiful. Through it, I've learned much about myself as well as the other members of my family. However, when our housemates got pregnant with child number two, we knew the time had come to seek out our own place.

Jamie had been searching diligently online and found a house which would enable the girls to continue attending their current school. We immediately contacted our phenomenal realtor, Karen, for a tour. Karen has graciously helped us purchase three houses, each one smaller than the one that preceded it. This true ranch-style home is a dream for us: *no stairs*, and it meets the current needs of our family. We made an offer, a counteroffer, and another counteroffer. Finally, we agreed upon a price, signed a contract, and continued to move forward towards purchase.

Currently, the house is owned by a bank, which has expressly communicated on multiple occasions that it will not do anything to improve the condition of the property. We followed Karen's advice and agreed to have the house professionally inspected. Instead of thumbing through the yellow pages, we trusted Karen when she recommended Randy Adams.

A couple days later, Randy called me, and we agreed upon a date and time for the inspection. For three hours on a summer afternoon, I followed Randy around as he told me everything that needed to be fixed. The hot water heater needed to be replaced immediately. The whole house needed to be scraped and repainted. Radon needed to be mitigated and siding and soffits replaced. Finally, the bird that lives in the attic would have to find a new home. Honestly, the inspection was overwhelming. As someone who usually uses his hands to play catch and guitar and to write sentences, I am not gifted with a hammer or a circular saw or dealing with 220 volts of electricity.

When you spend three hours with someone, you have a lot of time to talk. Randy and I hit it off. We talked about church and writing and baseball. He told me that he spends a few nights a week at The K because he helps to manage the Sheridan's Frozen Custard stands. He gave me his business card and told me to call him the next time I was headed to the stadium.

So, tonight, I called Randy. He said that it was his wife's birthday and he would be gone for a portion of the game celebrating dinner with her, but he would get in touch with me when he returned.

* * * * *

Becca and Mary Kate are both students whom I have gotten to know by being their youth minister. They have an older brother and an older sister, Ricky and Emily, who were both in my youth ministry as well. Their mom is a huge Royals fan, and I know that when I choose to wear my Sunday best to church (i.e. a Royals' jersey), she always smiles and appreciates the heart behind the choice of clothing. Emily now lives in Texas and contacted Becca a few weeks ago. She told Becca that it would be a good idea for her to marry Eric Hosmer.

Becca agreed.

For the first few innings of the game, the four of us brainstormed ways that Becca could possibly meet Eric Hosmer. We also agreed that, since I am technically a minister, I could officiate the wedding ceremony. Kaylea strongly petitioned to be a junior bridesmaid. The brainstorming session finally settled upon the idea of having Becca sign a baseball with her name and cell phone number on it and throw it to Hosmer as he departed the field at the end of an inning. But my seats were in the upper deck. And on the third base side. I know I've got a decent arm, but I just wasn't certain I could throw a ball all the way to first base from my seat. And the clincher: no one had a baseball. For the remainder of the game, however, whenever Hosmer stepped up to the plate, we referred to him as Becca's boyfriend.

* * * * *

In the fifth inning, Randy texted me and told me of his seats on the first level, much lower, but not that much closer to first base. The four of us headed to meet with Randy, who was writing reports of that day's inspections on his laptop. Randy treated us to free ice cream, and for the next three innings we continued the discussion we started during my house inspection. I told him of the latest happenings and frustrations with the bank and how Craig the mortgage lender had worked a miracle to get us into this property. He smiled sympathetically and told me not to waste any time worrying about it.

Randy then told me the following story. His mom, Louise Adams, used to work for the Royals. In 1979, she started selling tickets at the ticket office as a temporary seasonal position. At the end of the year, the Royals liked her so much they offered her a position as an administrative assistant to someone else they had hired that same year: the director of promotions, Rush Limbaugh. Randy told me how Rush grew to be a family friend. He said that he didn't know Rush as his radio personality, but as a deeply caring, compassionate, and generous individual. Rush only stayed with the Royals through 1984. Louise continued to work for the team through 1996.

Louise had already decided to retire at the beginning of the 1997 season when she was diagnosed with a brain tumor in December of 1996. Somehow, Rush heard of Louise's malady and hospitalization.[30] On the air one day, Rush contacted Louise, asking his listeners to pray for her and send her good thoughts. He must have mentioned both her name and the hospital on the air,

---

30 Some of the details of this next part might be wrong. The Royals' were rallying and the noise muffled the conversation.

because their switchboard was soon completely inundated with phone calls. Louise was a celebrity.

Louise passed away in February of 1997, before the Royals front office could honor her with the autographed ball that all retirees receive. The Royals agreed to host the family dinner after the funeral in the Stadium Club, a fitting place for a woman who devoted the last portion of her life to the team.

The way that Randy spoke of Rush made me think two things. First, I really do think that Rush and I could be friends. I doubt that we would agree on much politically, but that doesn't mean we couldn't get along. I've got friends who root for the Yankees and friends who root for the Cardinals. If I can be a friend with people who don't root for the Royals, surely I can be a friend with a conservative political commentator.

Secondly and more importantly, there is something about baseball that provides space for friendships. Kaylea noticed it this evening, too.

One of the Toronto players singled late in the game, and she witnessed this player and Becca's boyfriend carry on a conversation while the Royals made a pitching change. On the way home she commented, "Dad, even though they were on opposite teams, it sure looked like those two guys were friends. I think that's neat that even though they are both trying to win, and neither one wants to lose, they know that it's more important to be a good friend."

This is also part of the good news of Jesus. He, too, calls us friends. That is a radical statement. We live in a culture that loves to drop names of acquaintances who have connections, who are famous, or who make us feel more important. For example, Mom is a good friend with Brad Pitt's mom. That statement is supposed to make me more important because I am only three degrees removed from Brad Pitt. It's the real-life version of the Kevin Bacon game. But it doesn't really mean anything.

However, when the Living Word who whispered you into being, who knows you completely, and who invites you to follow him calls you "friend"—*now that means something.* Being called friend removes the hierarchies of relationships that define our culture. Being called friend expresses trust and vulnerability and a willingness to learn and grow together. Being called friend expresses a commitment to walk with you through the valleys and deserts and home-purchasing experiences of life. This Jesus who calls us friends also calls us to go and make new friends, wherever we happen to be, letting them know that he calls them friend too.

* * * * *

As it turned out, the game went to extra innings. With two outs and the bases loaded in the bottom of the 11th inning, Becca's boyfriend singled to centerfield and the Royals' won 3-2.

For the remainder of the season, whenever I go to a game, I'm going to give Randy a buzz. In addition to the free ice cream, which of course was a nice bonus on this sweltering evening, I truly enjoyed making a new friend.

12

Sophie's Questions

June 21, 2011
Royals' Record: 31-41
My Record: 7-4

"In baseball, you pass along wisdom."
—Buck O'Neil

It was a near-perfect summer's eve—a mild 79 degrees with a gusty wind. Sophie had been waiting patiently to go to another game with me. A lot has happened in the world of Sophie since our last trip to The K. Somewhere, in the space between the two games, Sophie became a reader. She now intently focuses on words here, there, and everywhere—reading her way through the day. A quick stop at the grocery store to pick up milk can take twenty minutes as Sophie tries to read *everything* in sight.

* * * * *

The game started off with a bang. Eight pitches in the top half of the first inning and Luke Hochevar had three outs, including one strikeout. As the Royals were coming up to bat, Sophie asked, "Will we see fireworks tonight? I really, really, really want to see fireworks." And on the first pitch, Alex Gordon hit a towering drive to right field. One pitch, one Alex Gordon home run, a 1-0 lead. Sophie got her fireworks.

That is also the last part of the game I remember seeing for many innings.

* * * * *

Along with being a reader, Sophie is also an artist. She sees the world differently than I do. She picks up subtleties and nuances in life and processes them while she cuts and glues and colors and crafts. We brought a backpack full of paper and markers and crayons "in case I think of a project that I need to draw."

In the top of the second inning, Sophie pulled out her paper and crayons. With the crayons came the questions and random observations of a night at The K through the eyes of a 6-year-old. I started taking notes of her questions so I could remember them later. Unfortunately, some of them are lost due to poor shorthand skills, a fading memory, and the on-going conversations. Here is a semi-comprehensive list of Sophie's questions and observations. (It is best if these are read out loud.)

What are all the rules of baseball?
How many rules are in baseball?
Do you know all of them?
Are the rules hard?
What's the weirdest rule in baseball?
What's another weird rule in baseball?
How do the players get on the field?

If it's a secret entrance, how do you know about it?
Can I see the secret entrance some time?
Have you ever been on a tour of the stadium?
Where was I?
Will you take me on a tour sometime soon?
Why do they call him "Moose?"
What are some of the other nicknames?
Do you have any nicknames?
Do you see that guy carrying frozen lemonade in a cooler on his head?
When will the cotton candy guy come to us?
Do you like blue or pink cotton candy?
Do you see the "KC" on the back of the dirt circle on the field?
What's the white circle on the dirt circle? (Rosin bag)
How big would you be if you were on the giant TV?
Are there any bigger TVs in the whole wide world?
Why are there garage doors in that building?
How long does it take to mow the field?
How many people does it take to mow it?
Do they make the designs on the field on purpose? I like the curvy lines more than the straight lines.

Sometimes, when I eat cotton candy, I can taste the sugar crystals. Did God make sugar?

Did God make cavities?

Did God make bad things? I'm going to have to brush my teeth really good so I don't get any cavities.

How do you eat cotton candy without making your fingers sticky?

What does "retro" mean?
Is that why some people are dressed so funny?
Do you ever dress "retro?"

So, they are pretending it's like 20 years ago?

How old would you have been 20 years ago?

Are you "retro?"

Do you see all the colors in the stadium? I was thinking that when we get to Heaven, we'll see colors that we've never seen before, but I'm pretty sure we'll see lots of blue too. It's just such a good color. It's in the sky and on the Royals uniform too. I like all the blues. And the pinks.

Do you see the pink and purple on those clouds?

Do you see how the pink makes lines in the sky?

Why does it say "Sprint" everywhere? And "Pepsi?" And "Sonic?"

Do you like real Dr Pepper or Diet Dr Pepper better?

How come there are so many signs all over the place?

Why does it say "Hy-Vee Level?" Is there a grocery store?

Who was better, Frank White or George Brett?

Do you think Frank White can see us in our seats?

Do you see the waves in the fountains?

How do you make the fountains work?

Will there be more fireworks? I like how fireworks in the daytime look like sparkles.

Do you remember where we parked?

What is a base on balls?

What is a can of corn?

What does K stand for? (Kauffman)

Is a strike out a different kind of K even though it's made with the same letter?

Do you think the ballplayers get nervous?

Would you be nervous if you were a ballplayer?

Why does the wind blow so hard?

What is a tornado?

How far away is Joplin?

Have you ever seen a tornado?

Would you be scared if you were in a tornado?

I don't like seeing all the trash on the ground. Aren't we supposed to help take care of our planet?

If God is my Heavenly Father, and he's also Linnsey's Heavenly Father, does that make us sisters?

Is everybody on this planet just really brothers and sisters?

Is there anything we can do to make more fireworks?

* * * * *

In between all the questions and comments and discussion, there was a baseball game. Honestly, I don't think I saw much of anything that happened from the second inning on. The middle innings slipped away as Sophie had a lot that she wanted to know. I tried to answer all of her questions. I figure that's pretty much my job as Dad—Question Answerer Supreme.

At this point, I looked up and saw that it was already past Sophie's bedtime. Alex Gordon was stepping up to the plate, and I knew that Sophie really wanted to see more fireworks. We started walking down the stairs and stood at the foot of the stairs watching his at bat. He hit another deep drive to right field that bounced off the top of the fence. He wound up at third base with an RBI triple. No fireworks for triples, though. What a shame.

* * * * *

Names are powerful. I think that names can shed light into someone's deepest meaning, the essence of who they are. I have noticed how people with the same name have shared mannerisms and traits that were too odd to be mere coincidence. The next time one of your friends who is a teacher is pregnant, watch how difficult it is for that person to name his or her child.

Sophie's name has a Greek origin. It means "wisdom."

In the book *The Shack*, the main character, Mack, has an encounter with Sophia, the personification of the Wisdom of God. The chapter (well, the whole book really) is beautifully written and exposes many of our presuppositions and assumptions about who God is. Over time, in ancient Hebrew thought, Wisdom came to be equated with a woman who speaks to the ordinary and everyday activities of life. She steps out into the streets amongst the busyness of the marketplace and calls out to anyone who will listen.[31] If you read through the writings of Proverbs, you can still hear the echoes of Wisdom's call to us today.

Wisdom cannot be taught like math or reading skills. Wisdom is not what is needed to pass a test or interview for a job. Wisdom comes through watching and listening, through reflection and contemplation, and through the courage to ask questions.

Unfortunately, for those of us living in the "ever-faster" culture, wisdom almost always comes slowly. Wisdom comes from both failure and success, though it seems that we learn better from failure. Wisdom grows when we pay attention to those who have lived long and well. Wisdom is very rarely found on television, though occasional glimpses are seen in the movies. Wisdom is not tweet-able and never found in fortune cookies or horoscopes.

More important than the questions we ask are the questions that Wisdom, through Jesus, asks us.

Why do you worry about clothes?

Who of you by worrying can add a single hour to his life?

Who is the greatest in the Kingdom of Heaven?

---
31 Proverbs 1.20; 8.1, 11-12.

What good will it be for a man if he gains the whole world, yet forfeits his soul?

You of little faith, why are you so afraid?

Why do you call me "Lord, Lord" yet do not do what I say?

Who do you say that I am?

If we would create space to sit with these questions, to allow them room in our souls, we would grow into the Wisdom of Jesus that lives free and unfettered in today's harried and harassed culture.

* * * * *

As we drove away from the stadium, Sophie's question barrage continued.

Dad, if there are fireworks in the last inning, will we still be able to see them?

Dad, can we read a book before bed?

Dad, what was your favorite part of the game? I think my favorite part is going to the game with you, because you answered my questions.

Dad, can we stop? I really have to go potty.

We stopped at a gas station, and the questions stopped too. While we were away from the radio, the Royals lost the game. However, it was, all in all, a near-perfect summer's eve.

13

The Transformations of Alex Gordon and Kaylea Bryan

June 24, 2011
Royals' Record: 31-44
My Record: 7-5

"You can do anything and you can be anything you want in this world, children. Remember that."
—Buck O'Neil

My oldest daughter, Kaylea, is in the middle of a transformation. Over the last year, she has gotten taller and stronger and, well, curvier. This transformation will affect every part of her: her emotions, her appearance, the way she processes and interprets information, even the way she interacts with me as a parent. In other words, Kaylea is growing up. She is no longer a little girl and is entering that world of adolescence faster than Apple can design a new iPhone.

Kaylea is also transforming into a ballplayer. She is starting to learn some of the various intricacies of the game—what it means to be a cut-off person, which infielder covers second base on a steal, and where to stand when a right-handed batter is hitting compared to when a left-handed batter is hitting. Having played all the positions in the outfield, as well as some innings at second base and shortstop, she is learning to appreciate the different responsibilities and perspectives from those positions. As a hitter, she doesn't swing at many bad pitches anymore, though she occasionally chases one over her head. And tomorrow Kaylea will be playing in her first fast-pitch softball tournament.

She's already informed me that she's nervous more than two hundred times. She has completely chewed her fingernails off and is asking a million questions a minute. What if they ask me to play third base? Will the pitchers throw the ball hard? Why does it have to be so early? What if it rains? What do you do when you're nervous? Do I talk a lot when I'm nervous?

Even though no real statistics are kept, Kaylea has got to be among the league leaders for on-base percentage. Over the last five games, Kaylea has been hit by some seven or eight pitches. She once told me, "When I see the ball coming at me, I close my eyes and try and move my head. Sometimes, though, I just forget to move my body, too." Add in a couple of walks and a couple of base hits, and it is the rare game that Kaylea doesn't get on base.

As we were driving to tonight's game, Kaylea asked me, "Dad, who is your favorite Royals' player this year?"

Without hesitation I replied, "Alex Gordon."

* * * * *

From my perspective, Alex Gordon wasn't ready when he was brought up to the major leagues. He was constantly fooled by off-speed pitches and struck out a lot. He played third base, but made numerous errors and actually had the lowest fielding percentage in the American League in 2008. The following couple of years were full of injury as he continued to struggle at the plate and in the field. Fans were restlessly awaiting Mike Moustakas to replace him at third base. I still cheered for Alex in those days. Part of being a person of faith means believing that the unseen will one day be a reality. Besides, his major league journey had only just started.

In 2010, the Royals moved Alex to left field, to see if he could make the switch from being an infielder to an outfielder. His defense improved dramatically. After the 2010 season, Alex worked with hitting-coach Kevin Seitzer (one of my all-time favorite Royals) who helped him overhaul his swing. And in 2011, everything clicked.

It doesn't really matter if Alex is hitting leadoff or clean up or anywhere else in the line-up; he's getting on base. When he's on base, he's stealing bases. When runners are in scoring position, he's having effective at bats, moving them around and driving them in. There's simply no one else I'd rather see at the plate with the game on the line than Alex Gordon.

Perhaps, though, the better story is his defense in the outfield. Alex plays left field like a third baseman, charging the ball hard and releasing cannon-like throws back to the infield. As of the end of June, he is leading the American League in outfield assists. I've seen him throw out at least half-a-dozen people, and each time is a thrill.

Tonight's game was full of Alex Gordon. He had two hits, two runs, a walk, and two more outfield assists. Even Kaylea commented that the opponents should know not to test the arm of Alex Gordon; he's simply gonna throw them out. In the sixth inning,

Aramis Ramirez tried to stretch a single into a double. Alex fired a rocket to Chris Getz, who had to wait for a moment or two before he could actually tag Ramirez out. Kaylea jumped to her feet and screamed.

For four seasons, Alex Gordon was barely average. Many fans grumbled at the mention of his name and his lack of production. They saw the potential of what he could do in college and the minor leagues, but he had failed to produce at the major league level. This year, Alex Gordon's transformation is finally visible for everyone to see. He is doing everything Kansas City Royals fans have been hoping he'd do. He is the Royals version of Charlie Hustle, giving everything he's got in every play, crashing into walls, taking out second basemen with slides, playing the game all-out. Alex Gordon is hands-down my favorite player to watch this year, and more people are jumping on my bandwagon with every game.

* * * * *

When one first starts to play baseball, there is much to learn. How to hold the ball. How to throw. How to run the bases so you don't run into the outfield grass. What pitches to swing at and when is a good time not to swing. When to throw to what base. How to bunt. How to steal. How to avoid getting hit by a pitch. How to catch pop-ups. How to react after you strike out. Growing into a ballplayer is a difficult and protracted process.

Growing into a follower of Jesus is also a long, challenging process.

The Scriptures only talk about transformation a little bit. Transformation is a ridiculously unhurried and unscripted process. Transformation means growing into the people whom God whispered and dreamed into being and lasts well into eternity.[32] Transformation is also a painful process, much like creating a diamond, a pearl, or a ballplayer.

Pierre Teilhard de Chardin once wrote:

> Above all, trust in the slow work of God. We are quite naturally impatient in everything to reach the end without delay. We would like to skip the intermediate stages.
>
> We are impatient of being on the way to something unknown, something new. And yet, it is the law of all progress that it is made by passing through some stages of instability—and that it may take a very long time.
>
> Above all, trust in the slow work of God, our loving vine-dresser.[33]

Transformation does not happen when everything is going your way. Transformation happens when nothing is going your way. Transformation can happen in life's crucible, when the stresses of bills, the pressures of work, and the tensions of relationships pull at one's soul. Unfortunately, in the middle of trying to live life, we are often too distracted to realize the potential for transformation.

Transformation begins when, in the midst of the trial and the struggle, we intentionally choose to trust God, to worship God, and to lean into God. It continues when we choose to love and serve others, especially when we don't feel like it. When we suspend judgment and offer grace, when we weep with others instead of offering advice, when our sighs are our prayers, when our questions and doubts are more than our answers, when we

---

[32] Benson's first book was *Between the Dreaming and the Coming True*. In it, he explores the concept of God whispering us into being, and us living out God's dreams.
[33] http://www.willmancini.com/2010/09/above-all-trust-in-the-slow-work-of-god.html, accessed June 2011.

feel the weight of the crosses we bear—these are all lessons in transformation.

It is hard to enjoy the process of transformation from a temporal perspective. No one volunteers to endure trial after trial. No one wants their faith and perseverance to be tested. And no one knows what the finished product or outcome is really going to be.

We cling to the little faith we have.

We muster enough hope for the day.

But we are frail creations who get distracted and discouraged and defeated.

Trapped in the present, we can't see how God is working in us for all of eternity.

The process of transformation is the outworking of the Spirit in our lives, not something that we can accomplish by our own strength or merit. It is our job to trust that God does, in fact, know what He's doing.

* * * * *

My sophomore year at Kickapoo High School was the last year I played competitive baseball. I wasn't very big compared to the other guys on my team. My growth spurt was still another eighteen months away, and it would be ten more years before I would start to put on any real weight. At almost every practice, Coach would yell at me.

"Throw harder!"

"Move faster!"

"Is that all you've got? Give me more!"

"Keep running!"

"Again! Again! Do it again!"

After one practice, the JV Coach approached me and quietly

whispered in passing, "He only yells at the ones he loves." When I learned that, my efforts increased another hundredfold. I don't know if there were any *tangible* results for my labors, but toward the end of the season, I remember Coach patting me on the back and saying, "Good job." He had noticed.

The Spirit of God transforms us because He loves us. We are a beautiful mess of hypocrisies and conundrums and paradoxes. The Spirit leads us to see Truth through bizarre and unusual experiences, through friends, and through the daily living of life. The Spirit gently—and sometimes not-so-gently—tears down our walls of ignorance and apathy and replaces them with love and compassion. The Spirit patiently, long-sufferingly waits for us to say, "I'm tired of doing this on my own." This is when the all-sufficient grace of Christ renews our hearts and attitudes.

* * * * *

I truly love watching Alex Gordon play baseball this year. He has matured into a top-notch, five-tool player: speed, power, average, arm, and defense. I love seeing how his hard work, determination, and perseverance are finally paying off.

In the bottom of the ninth inning, with the Royals down by two runs, two runners in scoring position, and two outs, Alex stepped up to the plate. Kaylea and I knew something good was going to happen. We were screaming and clapping and willing him to win the game with one swing of the lumber. With the count 1 – 1, Alex hit a slider sharply up the middle, an apparent game-tying single. However, Cubbies shortstop Starlin Castro made a great play followed by a great throw to get Alex out at first by a step.

Game over. Royals lost. There was no joy in Mudville—or Kansas City, for that matter.

Alex Gordon hasn't finished his transformation. It is going to be a delight watching him grow into one of the elite players in the majors—I can only dare to hope that he will be a Royal for life.

*****

On the morning of the softball tournament, the coach found Kaylea and told her that she would be hitting leadoff. As if she were not nervous enough already. So much for getting a manicure anytime in the next two or three years. If you got close enough to her, you could actually hear her stomach churning.

In the bottom of the first inning, the umpire called for the batter. She chewed on a couple more knuckles on her way up to the plate. I asked one of the other dads if he thought she was going to get plunked. The first pitch was a ball outside. On the second pitch, she took a good swing but missed. The pitcher let go of the third pitch, and it headed straight for Kaylea's head.

She took a step backwards and ducked. The ball completely missed her.

It was the first time all season that she has evaded being hit by a pitch.

Two of the other dads looked at me and chuckled. One quipped, "Hey! Look who's been practicing throwing a ball at his daughter!" We laughed together. Kaylea walked, stole second base, and scored a run on a hit by a friend.

Along with her transformation into a young woman, Kaylea has also started her transformation into a ballplayer. Well, kind of. After one of the ballgames in the tournament, Kaylea said, "Maybe next year I'll take horse riding lessons instead of playing softball."

Her transformation into who God whispered her into being will continue.
And so will Alex's.
And so will mine.

14

Major League Lessons: Kevin Seitzer

Played for KC Royals from 1986 – 1991
Hitting Instructor for KC Royals 2009 - Present
Tied MLB Record of 207 hits as a Rookie
Two Time All-Star
Played in 1997 World Series with Cleveland Indians

Career Stats:

AB	Runs	Hits	AVG
5278	739	1557	.295

October 20, 2011

I am sitting in the lobby of Mac-N-Seitz, one of the premier baseball and softball training facilities in the Midwest, because Kevin Seitzer called me.[34] On a couple occasions, I had left mes-

---
34 www.macnseitz.com

sages for Mr. Seitzer requesting an interview for this book, but I honestly didn't expect him to call me. I had even considered scheduling a hitting lesson—which would have been so cool—until I found out that none of his available times really fit my schedule. Yesterday, however, he called. Last night, I didn't sleep. You see, Kevin Seitzer is one of my personal Royals heroes.

I arrived at Mac-N-Seitz a few minutes early so I could set up and hopefully get rid of my junior-high-ish jitters. Mr. Seitzer walked in and greeted me warmly, shaking my hand. I gave him a quick introduction, hoping to convince him that I wasn't completely crazy. "I'm here on a mission from God, to write a book about baseball, faith, and this year's Kansas City Royals."[35] I took it as a sign to start the interview when he didn't run away after my introduction. I later learned that he has had five knee surgeries, and he probably decided it was less painful to endure some of my questions than to try to escape.

I asked the first question purely out of curiosity, "What kind of bat did you use?"

"Louisville Slugger, 33.5 inches long, 32 ounces—cupped and flamed, a C271. If you were gonna hit the ball hard, the bat needed some mass." When I got home, I called Louisville Slugger to see how much it would cost to obtain a Kevin Seitzer model bat. They told me that I needed to be somebody important in order to be able to fulfill that request. It wasn't the first time this season I have heard those words. Oh well, moving on.

On July 1, 1990, Dad took a couple of friends and me to a Royals game. The Royals hosted the Detroit Tigers, and Seitzer was the leadoff hitter in the bottom of the first inning. I asked Mr. Seitzer what he remembered about that at-bat.

"It was against Jack Morris. The first pitch was a change-up.

---
35 I didn't use these exact words.

The second pitch was a slider. I didn't see the third pitch until it was two feet from my face. I had enough time to duck down a little. The ball caught the helmet squarely and sent it flying; I fell to the dirt unconscious. I played the next day but had a case of the 'flinchies' for the remainder of the season. I actually considered retiring but had only been in the league for three years. During the off-season, I had to do some extra mental work to be ready to stand in and face the pitcher the following season. You can't be a success if you're scared you're not going to see the next pitch.

"A couple of years later, it happened again. Facing Yankees pitcher Melido Perez, I got hit just below the eye and had six facial-bone fractures. Immediately, I knew what I had to do. I called home, asking friends and family and prayer warriors to pray for me. I asked them to pray that I would not be afraid, that I would get back to the game quickly. I knew that I couldn't make it through this on my own strength and ability. That night, I iced my face to get the swelling down, hoping to get my contact in the next morning.

"When I got to the clubhouse the next day, I walked straight for the lineup card. When I saw that my name wasn't on it, I ripped it down and went straight to the manager. I yelled at him and demanded to be in the lineup. After I vented, he calmed me down and told me that the doctors hadn't released me yet to play. I had to have a C-flap installed on my helmet for protection before I could play again. Two days later, I was back in the lineup, facing Sterling Hitchcock. When I stepped in the box, I had no fear. I could literally feel the effects of the prayers. I knew Sterling as a friend and believer, and he very graciously walked me on four pitches outside.

"One year later, I got hit in the head for the third time. This one hit my temple and hurt even more than the ball from Perez, even though no bones broke. Having been in this situation before, I knew what I had to do. I prayed hard, and I called on others to pray for me again. Two days later, I was back in the box and went three for four in the game. I experienced the peace of God in the midst of my pain."

In fact, Kevin Seitzer has experienced almost everything possible in the major leagues. He was voted to two All-Star teams, won the 1997 ALCS with the Cleveland Indians, and played in the World Series, losing to the Florida Marlins in seven games. He has known the joys of a fantastic season, as well as the heartbreak of the business side of the game, being released by a couple of teams. Seitzer learned that more important than performing for God on the field is surrendering to Him completely in all of life.

"It's so easy for ballplayers—for anyone—to get caught up in unrealistic expectations and the cares of this world, to put too much emphasis on results. Faith teaches us to focus on now, today, not to dwell on the past or on those things that aren't in my control or responsibility. When I do what I can to obey God, to live by His Word, and trust Him with the results—phenomenal things can happen. And phenomenal things can't always to be measured in numbers, either.

"God gave me a gift, and I've had so much fun playing ball and passing on my education and experiences to others. Even with the travel, and the hard part of being away from family, I can say that there's nothing else I'd rather do."

Since 2009, Seitzer has been the hitting instructor for the Royals. He is both wise and patient, understanding when to work with young hitters and when to give them space. He understands the hard work that is necessary to succeed in the major leagues. He also knows that it is imperative that a hitter never stop learning, always being willing to hear the words and advice of others instead of going at it alone.

I asked, "Who was your favorite person to coach and watch this season?"

"That's like asking me which of my children is my favorite. Every day, every pitch, I'm right there with nine guys, nine of my boys, wanting them to succeed, to do their best. How can you say that any of your children is your 'favorite?'

"Having said that, I have really enjoyed watching Alex Gordon this season. Last year, in the off-season, Alex worked so hard. He was diligent and put in the time and practice and expected good things to happen. However, two weeks into Spring Training, things weren't clicking yet. I reminded him to be patient and to keep focusing on what we'd worked on. I went away for a couple of days to watch one of my sons play and came back to this message: 'Go check on Gordo.'

"I found him in his street clothes looking completely devastated. We went into the video room and closed the door. We watched some footage together, and then I shared my story. And then, I shared about Jesus. I told him that it's about a real relationship, a real peace. Jesus is not a 'to-do' list or just a bunch of rules, but the only one who can ground you and walk with you through life's hardest times. And right there, Alex Gordon prayed and started following Jesus.

"Everyone could see the change in Gordo. They even talked about it in the clubhouse. From my perspective, I could see that Alex was relaxing, that he was free; it looked like 2,000 pounds had just been lifted off of his back. And I think that Gordo would say that his success this season is definitely a result of all of his hard work, but also the working out of God's glory in his life."

"You are the first person 'of the media' I've shared this with." (Secretly, I was thrilled to be called a "media" person.)

We both had tears in our eyes at the end of the story. I told Mr. Seitzer how much I, too, had enjoyed watching Alex Gordon play this season, sharing with him some of my stories as a fan.

Kevin Seitzer is a normal person, with feelings, strengths, weaknesses, fears, and successes—just like every other ballplayer. He has shared the gifts and talents that God has given him, experiencing a full life in the major leagues. He tied major league records for hits in a rookie season (207) and number of hits in a nine-inning game (6). He has experienced the pain and limitations of knee surgeries and spent the second half of his career icing one part of his body or another. He has been in All-Star games and released in the middle of a season. Through it all, Seitzer has learned that it's not about him and his abilities, but about surrendering completely to an amazing God.

"Baseball is a game of numbers, where everything is measured. Sometimes, though, not even numbers can accurately describe the picture. My 'make-up' isn't defined by just my talent and abilities or by my numbers. I am a whole person, a normal human being. God isn't interested in my numbers; God is interested in the whole package—in all of me."

Seitzer's gift isn't reserved for major leaguers only. He also works with area kids at Mac-N-Seitz, sharing in the joys of their games and stories as well. Seitzer's faith lives in the passing on of his baseball education to others, and it shines as brightly as the stars in the heavens.

15

Buck O'Neil Day

July 9, 2011
Royals' Record: 36-53
My Record: 7-6

"The triple. That's my favorite play.
Someone hits a triple
Everyone's running.
The whole field bursts to life, man,
Best play in baseball."
—Buck O'Neil

It is almost the All-Star break. The Royals have a game tonight and tomorrow before the three-day vacation. As of right now, they are 17 games below .500—three games worse than last year's team.

Tonight's game is the celebration of Buck O'Neil's 100th birthday.[36] Buck spent the last fifteen years of his life as an ambassador for the Negro Leagues, including overseeing the construction of

---

36 Buck's real birthday is November 13, 1911. He passed away on October 6, 2006.

the Negro Leagues Baseball Museum, now located near 18th and Vine in downtown Kansas City, Missouri. His brother, Warren, threw out the first pitch at tonight's game, and stories about Buck were shared on the scoreboard throughout the game. Buck loved to tell stories about the amazing men with whom he played ball in the Negro Leagues.

A few years ago, a friend gave me some really good tickets to the Royals game, down on the lower deck on the third base side. Seated only a couple sections over and a few rows closer to the field was Buck O'Neil, in a chair on the aisle. A part of me wanted to rush over and get an autograph and attempt to say something intelligent. I watched as others younger than I cautiously approached Buck with baseballs and t-shirts and scraps of paper, obtaining autographs and exchanging simple conversations. When I finally screwed up my courage to head his way, he wasn't in his seat, and he didn't return for the remainder of the game. I missed my only chance to hear a story in person.

Joe Posnanski followed Buck for a year, traveling all over the country, going to baseball games, promoting the Negro League Baseball Museum, and petitioning for Negro League players to be admitted into the Hall of Fame. Posnanski's year with Buck turned into one of my favorite baseball books, *The Soul of Baseball*, a beautiful portrait of Buck's passionate and gentle spirit. Buck's contagious joy could put a positive spin on anything. In one story, Joe and Buck were at a game in Houston, and the right fielder tossed a ball into the stands at the end of an inning. As Joe tells it:

> Two people reached for the ball. One was a thirty-something man in a sports coat and a loosened tie. The

other was a boy, probably ten or eleven. The boy wore a Houston Astros jersey with the number 7 on it.

The boy and the man both stretched for the ball, but the man was taller and he had the better angle. He caught the ball. He threw his arms up in the air, as if he was signaling a touchdown. The man was happy. The boy was glum, and he sat down.

"What a jerk," I said.

"What's that?" Buck muttered.

"That guy down there caught the ball and won't give it to a kid sitting right behind him. What a jerk."

"Don't be so hard on him," Buck mumbled. "He might have a kid of his own at home."

That stopped me cold. A kid of his own. I had not thought of that.

Buck's optimism never failed him. Hope never left him. He always found good in people.

"Wait a minute," I said to Buck. "If this jerk has a kid, why didn't he bring the kid to the ballgame?"

"Maybe," Buck said without hesitation, "his child is sick."

And I realized that no matter how hard I tried, I would never beat Buck O'Neil at this game.[37]

* * * * *

Tonight was the first time this season that my entire family attended a game. Kaylea had already started with the questions, Sophie really wanted fireworks, and Jamie and I were trying not to

---

37 Joe Posnanski, *The Soul of Baseball: A Road Trip Through Buck O'Neil's America* (New York: HarperCollins Publishers, 2007) pp. 4-7.

melt from the oppressive heat. The first two innings lasted more than an hour, and another hour passed before the following two were completed. The game was dragging along at a snail's pace, and I noticed that I was anxious for the game to hurry up and get moving.

There was no other place I needed to be.

There was nothing more important I needed to be doing.

If I was honest, there was no other place that I would rather be than there at the stadium.

If I could have handpicked three people to join me at tonight's game, these were the three people I would choose over anyone else in the world.

Two days ago, we were supposed to close on our new home. Three days ago, we lost the house—the one that started the argument between Jamie and me. We were now back to square one. The last 72 hours had been quite emotional and difficult. Maybe God knew that I needed a long evening to sit back, to breathe, to allow the game to speak healing into my hurt places.

*****

I recently visited the Negro Leagues Baseball Museum. I watched a beautiful video narrated by James Earl Jones and learned that the 1985 Royals were not the first baseball World Champions in Kansas City—the Monarchs beat them to it 61 years earlier. There were stories of names that I knew: Henry Aaron, Willie Mays, Jackie Robinson, Ernie Banks. There were stories of names I had forgotten: Cool Papa Bell, Satchel Paige, Josh Gibson, Rube Foster. And there were stories that needed to be told over and over again. Toni Stone was the first woman to play professional baseball—in the Negro Leagues. J.C. Wilkinson invented night baseball in the Negro Leagues years before it appeared in the Major Leagues. Stories of hate and ignorance and prejudice. Stories of hope and love and forgiveness. It is important to remember all of these stories. If we forget, it will once again be easy to create divisions, to superficially judge others, to lose sight of the fact that we are all brothers and sisters.

It is easy to see divisiveness growing in our country. We choose to live in neighborhoods where everyone is alike. Larger cities have ethnic enclaves named for the population: Chinatown, Little Italy, Irishtown. Immigrants come to our melting pot culture and create communities of safety and comfort, finding ways to translate their culture into the American Dream. Now, in New York City, more than 100 different countries are represented and 170 languages are spoken. Los Angeles is home to the largest Korean population outside of Korea. When we live in fear of those who look different on the outside and speak with accents, it doesn't take much for that fear to turn from misunderstanding into hate.[38]

Buck O'Neil knew hate. He heard the slurs and the jeers. Because of the color of his skin—something over which he had no control—life wasn't easy or fair. In a room full of young kids, one little boy asked Buck why it was that blacks and whites hated each other. Buck said,

"Son, there never was a time
Everybody hated everybody.
Never so.
Always good white folk.
Always good black folk.
Remember, son.
Don't let hate fill your heart.
Always more good people

---

38 The movie *Crash* does a wonderful job of telling this story.

*Than bad
In this world."*[39]
We need to remember this too.

* * * * *

When I was a boy, my Papaw owned a farm-and-home store in southeast Missouri. One of my earliest memories is walking into the store and seeing Melvin. Melvin was one of the first African-Americans hired on equal status with a white man in Mississippi County, Missouri. For some reason, I was immediately attracted to Melvin. I could see Papaw and Uncle Mike when the day's work was done, but any time I went to the store, I was there to see Melvin and follow him around. From the cash register to the shop to sweeping the floor, wherever Melvin was, I was. People joked and called me his "white shadow." I didn't care. All I knew was that Melvin was a friend. And fifteen years later, when I was getting married, Melvin drove his family across Missouri to attend the ceremony.

The Scriptures say, "In Christ's family, there can be no division into Jew and non-Jew, slave and free, male and female. Among us, you are all equal."[40] In Jesus, we are all the same. We are equals.

Thankfully, we now see this on the field. Baseball is truly a cross-cultural sport, with players from numerous countries around the world.

I wish church would catch up with baseball, however. Sunday morning is still the most segregated time in our culture. There are still churches that use Scripture to promote racism, classism, and sexism. We send women as missionaries to plant churches and

---
39 Posnanski, *The Soul of Baseball*, pp. 191-192.
40 Galatians 3.28, Today's Message

preach in other countries, but don't allow them to have leadership roles within our churches in the United States. Equality is one of the unalienable rights upon which our country was founded. But what does equality look like? Equality doesn't mean communism or Marxism or any other "ism." Equality means that we are all free, regardless of race or gender, to use the gifts God has granted us with responsibility and joy. Every single person is created in the image of God. There is no hierarchy—as Paul writes, we are all to submit to one another out of love and respect for Christ. If we are truly living out love, the playing field is equal for all.

* * * * *

Les Norman played in 78 games for the Royals from 1995 to 1996. Every year, he hosts a free clinic for those playing baseball and softball in the Greenwood Sports Association. I thought the clinic would be a great time to sharpen Kaylea's skills, so I agreed to go with her on the rainy Saturday morning. While we were registering, she noted that there weren't many girls attending. In fact, Kaylea was one of only two girls at the clinic. Ashley, a teammate who had just moved to Missouri from Alaska, also was present.

Les gathered all the kids in the outfield for some introductory remarks. He joked and held the crowd's attention before saying that what he would teach today would help everyone, whether they played baseball or softball. One of the boys loudly questioned, "Softball? Oh, come on, that's not very hard."

Immediately, Les spoke in defense of fast-pitch softball. He explained that, because of the distance between the mound and the plate, fast-pitch softball is actually harder than baseball. He commented that the girls who play fast-pitch are every bit the athletes as the boys who play baseball. Finally, he said that there was no room for sarcasm or cynicism for someone else simply because they are a different gender. The boy was silent for the rest of the clinic. Kaylea looked at me and smiled.

* * * * *

Tonight, the Royals played the Detroit Tigers. The Royals scored one in the first, three in the second, and five in the third, thanks to Alex Gordon's home run to centerfield. Sophie got her fireworks wish again. Luke Hochevar struggled with the strike zone, however, and was pulled before he could make it to the fourth inning. The Tigers battled. In the top of the fifth inning, the Royals were leading 9-6.

Old Royals fans waited for the team to find a way to lose the game. For years now, faithful fans have hoped and rooted, only to see the boys in blue continue to come up short. I could sense that feeling of anxious dread rising in me. *Not tonight,* I whispered to myself, *Not on Buck's night.* And then I imagined what Buck would say. I think it would go something like this:

"These boys sure are a lot of fun to watch.

Don't you give up on them,

They've got a lot of heart.

Keep on believing.

No harm comes

From hoping,

Wishing for the best."

And he would have been right.

For the first few months of the season, Alcides Escobar, the shortstop who amazed us with his glove and arm, left us longing for something—*anything*—at the plate. His batting average hovered under the Mendoza line.[41] However, for the last month, he has gone on a tear and is hitting a respectable .250. In the bottom of the sixth inning, with two out and two on, Escobar ripped a triple to left field. Buck would have been proud. He is right; there is nothing more exciting than a triple. Those runs were the nails in the coffin. The next three innings took almost no time, and the Royals won 13-6.

*****

As the dad of a couple of girls, and as someone who is familiar with the rampant sexism within the evangelical Christian culture, I want to teach my girls that they are free, they are equal, in Christ. Their job is to learn to love and see the good in all people.

Major League Baseball ultimately listened to Buck O'Neil, and members of the Negro Leagues were admitted to the National Hall of Fame in Cooperstown. The church could learn a thing or two by listening to Buck as well.

---

41 The Mendoza line is an expression that comes from shortstop Mario Mendoza whose lifetime batting average defines incompetent hitting. Mendoza's lifetime average was .215. However, when people reference the "Mendoza Line," they usually mean .200.

16

Major League Lessons: Les Norman

Played in 78 Games for KC Royals in 1995 - 96
1993 Royals' Minor League Player of the Year
1993 AA All-Star Game MVP

Career Stats:

AB	Runs	Hits	3B	RBI	BB	AVG
89	15	15	1	4	12	.169

I was driving home from work a few months ago and noticed my friend, Bart, playing catch with his son in their backyard. I pulled over my car and immediately joined in. After a few moments of small talk, Bart commented on my Royals' shirt, "We're having a former Royals player and his family over for dinner tonight." My eyes nearly bugged out of my head as he continued, "Les Norman is a friend of mine, and they are joining us for dinner. He's a believer, you know. Got a great heart and love for the game." I confess, part of me thought about crashing the dinner party just for an opportunity to meet a former major leaguer.

As providence would have it, I got the opportunity to meet Les after the baseball and softball skills clinic. Kaylea asked him to autograph her Royals t-shirt (which she now wears with great pride, pointing out the autograph to everyone), and I told him about this book project. "Is there any chance I could interview you?" He agreed immediately. We met today in a corner table at a local grocery store.

The first question was supposed to be an easy question: "What is your favorite baseball book?" The genre of baseball literature continues to rapidly grow every year, as new biographies, autobiographies, and novels are introduced every spring. "I've read a lot of baseball books," Les replied, "But how can a book replace a thirty-minute conversation with Pete Rose? How can a book compare to learning a defensive secret from Ken Griffey, Jr.? How can a book describe what it's like to stand in and face a 98 mph fastball from Randy Johnson?" He had a good point. As he said these words, I considered scrapping this whole project. He continued, "I remember walking up the steps from the clubhouse and seeing Kauffman Stadium for the first time, thinking, 'This is what I've dreamed about.' That was one of my favorite moments, one of my sharpest memories, in all of baseball. It's hard to compare those experiences to a book."

Les is only a couple of years older than me and is in terrific shape. I noticed the bandage on his leg and asked about what had happened. "I slid on third base in a softball game. It tore my leg up." Oddly enough, I've got the same scar from the same softball complex. "Sliding in shorts is never smart."

He then showed me his right collarbone, which appeared to not be connected to anything. "I'm stronger now than I've ever been, and it doesn't cause me any pain or hinder my abilities." I was confused. I was under the impression that Les had retired because of shoulder injuries. "I ended my career on my terms. I wanted to raise a family with my wife. I didn't want to raise a family from the road. I wasn't going to be the guy I felt sorry for, the one I watched call home every night with tears in his eyes, wishing he could watch a pee-wee league game or help on a Boy Scout project while chasing some dream.

"It's hard to live the baseball life. Around 80% of retired players get divorced because they don't know how to share life with their spouse or kids. They are gone half of the year, doing their own thing, and now have to return to 'normal.' Many fans think that money and the material perks make life easy, make it worthwhile. These same fans buy all the memorabilia, placing the players on a pedestal. They don't understand that the players are just human beings, normal people whose gifts and talents place them in the public eye. There is a near epidemic of professional athletes who commit suicide after their careers are over because they don't know who they are. They don't know how to live a 'normal' life.

"Because of my faith, I know who I am and whose I am. I was not defined by my performance on the field; I am just a guy saved by the love of Jesus, who is blessed enough to get the opportunity to make a living playing baseball. My faith has kept me humble, kept me grounded.

"I remember being the fifth outfielder in low-A ball in Wisconsin, shortly after I became a believer. I committed then to being a 100% team player. If they needed someone to keep the books, I'd do it. If they needed someone to catch bullpens or chase foul balls, whatever was needed to help my teammates, I'd do it. It was in low-A that I learned what it meant to serve others. Money, fame, and success will only grant temporary happiness. I discovered more joy as I learned to focus on God. When I quit obsessing about myself, I was free to become who I was born to be—and my baseball career took off. Within two seasons, I was in the majors. So many kids today are under tremendous pressure from their parents who define success as winning. One of the most important things I'm trying to teach kids as a coach is to have fun playing the game. When you are able to take your eyes off yourself and your performance, you'll play better. It's really a paradox.

"It was because of the sacrifice and love of so many other people, from my mom and wife to numerous coaches, that I was able to make it to the majors. When I'd start to doubt or be afraid, their example and faith in me strengthened me, encouraged me. Sometimes, professional athletes exist in a world of 'entitlement,' full of themselves and convinced that they got to where they are on their own. Part of being human and an athlete is the constant reminder of sharing life together. That's what I miss most about the game, the camaraderie of my teammates—whether it's playing cards in the locker room during a rainout or sitting on the floor in an airport waiting for a plane. Baseball is a game where individuals only succeed when a team comes together. When your focus is self, you miss the chance for life, for relationship—all the good stuff."

Les shared stories of being called up into the majors, of how he was set up and tested by his coaches in AAA during the game. We laughed as he told of crazy rookie initiations, from signing autographs in women's clothing to the "Three Man Lift," and getting pranked by George Brett. He was grateful for veterans like Brent Mayne and Jeff Montgomery and Mark Gubicza who took care of the rookies, even when managers hated them.

I asked, "If you could have four players from any era over to your house for dinner, who would you choose?"

"Babe Ruth. How could a guy eat 20 hot dogs a day, be in horrible physical shape, make the transition from pitcher to outfield, and make such a remarkable impact on the game? What kind of things went through his head? I'd also invite Pete Rose. This guy compiled more than 4,200 hits—day in, day out. Consistent. What a tough and focused approach. He definitely deserves to be in Cooperstown. I'd invite Jackie Robinson, because I'm humbled and amazed by his tenacity and his ability to thrive when no one else wanted him to succeed. Finally, Roberto Clemente. This is a guy who played the game the right way, for the right reasons. He died trying to serve others in need."

Today, Les does many things. He is first a husband and a dad who plays with Legos and takes evening walks in the neighborhood. He is a coach and teaches private lessons, passing along his knowledge and love of the game to the next generation. He coaches the Swing Builder Saints and emphasizes respect for authority ("Nine-year-olds have no place rolling their eyes at an umpire."), playing hard and, most importantly, having fun. He hosts a radio show on Tuesday nights on 810 AM WHB called "Breakin' the Norm," discussing behind-the-scenes, relevant issues of all sports for all ages. He is also an excellent public speaker who focuses on faith-based, motivational, and personal branding messages.

"Those who do best in baseball, just like those who do best in life, aren't afraid to fail. There's always another at bat, another game. You might strike out in your first three at bats, only to win the game on a bloop single to right field. For too long, I beat myself up, and absolutely nothing good can come from that. Faith teaches me to keep looking forward, that the time to live—to do—is now. Paul reminds us to leave the past behind and press on towards the goal, the prize that is Christ. Failure is just part of being human. God doesn't abandon me when I screw up, but enables me to get back in the game and try again.

"I still love Opening Day and walking out on the field. I love

Fantasy Camp and connecting with other guys who had baseball dreams, being the grunt for the Royal greats. But when I quit playing the game, I learned to go out with humility."

That's not something you hear every day, a professional athlete talking about humility. Humility leads to thankfulness, to gratefulness, to learning to see the joy in life. And humility helps keep everything in proper perspective, where playing with Legos with his boys is every bit the special memory as seeing Kauffman Stadium for the first time.

Les closed with a story about one of his best days in baseball.

"On September 4, 1995, I received my second call-up of the season; I was completely exhausted walking in the clubhouse doors. The Royals were in the playoff hunt and in prime wildcard position, which made the call-up even more exciting.

"As I entered the clubhouse, I walked in on a hitters meeting in progress. I simply sat down, having no idea who the pitchers were they were talking about, let alone how they would pitch me if I actually came in. If I did get in the game, keeping my knees from literally knocking together would have been my first agenda.

"That night, we played a double-header against the Toronto Blue Jays. The likes of Roberto Alomar, John Olerud, Ed Sprague, Carlos Delgado, Shawn Green, and others pressed my nerves to their limit. I didn't get in the first game, which was both a relief and a bummer, since I wanted to play so badly, yet I also wanted to take a twelve-hour nap.

"Riding on sheer adrenaline, I got ready for game two. I wasn't in the starting lineup. In the bottom of the eighth inning, we were down by a run, and the manager motioned to me. I think I tripped seventeen times from the middle of the dugout to the helmet rack, and immediately I forgot how to read numbers. I just grabbed a helmet and my bat, and asked hitting coach Greg Luzinski what this guy would throw me. 'He's a lefty that throws cutters inside, every time.'

"'Okay, what should I do?' I stammered.

"'Yank the sucker into the left field seats!'

"Sure thing. Easy enough. I walked up to the plate with Michael Tucker standing on second, Greg Gagne on first, one out, and the crowd was electric. I could literally *feel* the roar. The fans became my backbone. First pitch, borderline inside cutter, ball one. Stepped out and thought to myself, *That looked like 100 miles per hour!* Looked at the radar gun—84. *Wow, I had better get started early.* I stepped back in, and the crowd noise-level is now in the ballistic range. *Hit this next inside pitch as hard and far as you can to left field*, I told myself. The pitch came inside, but I got my foot down late. With an instant adjustment, I kept my hands inside the ball, and a hard ground ball shot off of my bat, just inside the first base bag and up the right field line.

"It was a combination of *Run as fast as you can!* with *Don't fall down!* As I rounded second, I saw the third base coach waving Gagne home, so I put my head down and bolted for third. Let's be aggressive.

"The throw goes home, everybody is safe, and the first thing I see are my teammates in the dugout. All the veterans standing and applauding, all the rookies I came up with jumping in front of the dugout, pointing at me, fist pumping, and giving me the greatest on-field moment of a lifetime. I almost threw up at third base on Ed Spragues' shoes. That would have made Plays of the Week for sure. My two RBIs gave us the lead, 8-7.

"Johnny Damon came up next and hit a bloop single to left. I scored that run and we went on to win by a score of 9-7. Euphoria can't begin to describe it. I slept great that night, not because I was a hero (Boone actually got the glory for that one, based on his decision to pinch-hit me at that time. After all, *he* was the Stanford genius), but most importantly, I felt like a member of the team. My rite of passage was complete. I was 'one of the guys.'

"That was my only extra-base hit in the big leagues. We all want careers that hold many moments like that, but I consider it a direct blessing from God that it's my only one. I can honestly say that it wasn't a moment about me—it was about team, contribution, and relationship. To be counted on, and to be able to deliver, for the team and for the 30,000 people in the stands who screamed their way into my skin and shared that victory.

"Some people talk about storybook endings. I have one. It's a small book, but it's in print, even if only in my internal bookstore. To this day, I reread that book often. It never gets old, never wears out, and the details are always fresh. For most people, one moment isn't very much; but to me, it's all I ever needed."

17

The Next Generation

August 15, 2011
Royals' Record: 50-71
My Record: 8-6

"In baseball, you play catch with your son. You teach him how to hold a bat, how to swing it, how to get under a pop-up, how to throw to the right base. You teach him how to run the bases. You teach him how to run back on a ball over his head. You teach him how to throw a curveball. You see what I'm saying?"
—Buck O'Neil

Kaleb is a Yankees fan. I try not to hold that against him.

Kaleb is the only male in a single-parent household. He has two younger sisters. I've never met his dad. I heard he lives somewhere in California, which sounds pretty nice come January or February. The only thing I've ever heard Kaleb say about his dad was, "I don't care about him." Life can be hard when you are the oldest male in your household as a high school freshman.

Kaleb is also in our youth group at church. A few months ago, after worship on Sunday, I called out to him and said something about playing catch. He told me he'd have to get a new glove. I would have given him one of my gloves except he is left-handed and I am not. A few weeks later, we had the opportunity to go to a local sporting goods store together and try on gloves. He picked one out, and I went back for it the next day. The storeowner tossed in a baseball for us as a gift.

I drove straight to Kaleb's house, which is only two minutes from my office. We threw until we couldn't throw any more. I recommended ice and Advil that evening. I went back the next day. And the next. Pretty soon, I started texting Kaleb on Saturday nights, "Bring your glove to church. We'll play catch after worship." Unfortunately, sometimes Kaleb is grounded from his phone and doesn't get my messages.

Playing catch is an important part of growing up. For years, Dad and I played catch every day when he got home from work. On warm days, Kaylea and I toss the ball while waiting for the school bus. Guys my age still get teary-eyed watching the last scene in *Field of Dreams* when Ray Kinsella (Kevin Costner) says, "Hey, Dad? You wanna have a catch?" Playing catch is a formative rite of passage.

I can understand why Kaleb is a Yankees fan. The Yankees have been in the playoffs or World Series almost every year as long as he's been alive. When everyday life is difficult and demanding, choosing a winning team to support feels pretty good. Besides, almost everybody looks good sporting pinstripes.

* * * * *

The New York Yankees.

The name itself deserves to be a sentence of its own. There is simply no other team like them.

They have won twenty-seven World Championships and forty American League Pennants. Since the Royals won their one-and-only World Series in 1985, the Yankees have won five and lost two others. Comparing the Yankees to the Royals is like comparing a rotary phone with an iPhone; they are two completely different entities.

The Yankees are in a class and generation by themselves. Even in a new stadium, they are the embodiment of tradition. There is no player name above the number on the back of the pinstriped jerseys. Many uber-competitive and obsessive fans are intimidated simply by the name of the team. Along with being steeped in tradition, they are also the fulfillment of the east coast mindset—bigger, better, faster, and *way* more expensive.

The Yankees 2011 payroll leads the majors at $196,854,630. The Royals 2011 payroll is last in the majors at $35,712,400. In fact, there are multiple combinations of two players on the Yankees who can cover the entire Royals' payroll.

The average age of the Yankees in tonight's game is, according to my rudimentary math, 32.6 years old. The average age of tonight's Royals' team is 24.6. This means that when the Yankees players were being tested for their driver's licenses, the Royals players were learning to write in cursive and memorizing multiplication tables.

Forty-three Yankee players and eleven Yankee managers have been inducted into the Baseball Hall of Fame. As a team, the Yankees have retired the numbers of sixteen people and are waiting to retire number forty-two with Mariano Rivera.

The Royals have only one player and one broadcaster in the Hall of Fame.[42] The team has retired the numbers of four players, including Jackie Robinson.

* * * * *

For Easter, I gave Kaleb the Yankees fan a ticket to join me at tonight's game. We've been talking about it ever since. On the way to pick up Kaleb, I called Benson the Author and told him that I was headed to the ballpark. He was slightly jealous. Mantle, Maris, Berra, and other pinstriped players were his childhood heroes. I told him we would keep score for him and send him the scorecard.

We arrived at the stadium in time to watch the Bronx Bombers live up to their name in batting practice, hitting numerous monstrous home runs. After batting practice, Kaleb the Yankees fan and I headed over to the Royals bullpen to watch Felipe Paulino and new catcher Salvador Perez warm up. We watched how Paulino gripped his pitches, focusing on working the corners and throwing the ball down in the zone. After the national anthem, Paulino motioned to us and tossed us the ball he had used during warm-ups. Kaleb played with that ball for the remainder of the game.

On the way to our seats, we stopped to pick up a scorecard, but the stadium had already sold out. This is known as the Yankee effect. Wherever the team travels, fans of the pinstripes come out of the woodwork wearing numbers and jerseys of players current and retired, selling out stadiums, and buying all the scorecards.

The day of the game, a friend sent me a link to an article

---

42 George Brett and Denny Matthews are currently in the Hall of Fame. It is my not-so-humble opinion that Frank White and Dan Quisenberry should also be inducted.

positing that the Royals are a better team than the Yankees.[43] It was creatively written and entertaining and, I think, spot-on. The Royals are the team of the next generation baseball fan. They are young and looking to find their place in the annals of baseball history, alongside the greats of the game.

Tonight, Derek Jeter had his 218th three-hit game. Royals second baseman, Johnny Giavotella, also had a three-hit game; it was his first.

Yankees catcher and designated hitter (DH), Jorge Posada, has played in more than 1800 games. Royals veteran DH, Billy Butler, has played in 650 games; rookie catcher Perez was playing his fifth game.

In tonight's game, every player in the Royals' line-up had at least one hit. Two Yankees' players went hitless.

The Royals battled, but the Yankees came out on top. Kaleb was ecstatic. We witnessed Mariano Rivera recording his 590th save in the ninth inning, leaving no hope for a comeback. By season's end, most likely, Rivera will be the major-league leader in saves recorded. We saw history in the making.

* * * * *

I have played soccer and loved it, especially the seasons when Dad was the coach. I have played golf and still love it, actually watching portions of the professional tournaments on television over the weekends. I have played basketball—and poorly at that—and now have a new anterior cruciate ligament because of it. But no other sport I have played compares with baseball.

I've heard people talk about the future of baseball, how it's

---

[43] http://www.theatlantic.com/entertainment/archive/2011/05/why-the-royals-are-a-better-baseball-team-than-the-yankees/239085/, accessed on May 30, 2012.

"too slow" and can't hold the interest and attention of the video game generation. I understand how some fans were burned by the strike in 1994. I also understand how some fans struggle with the steroid issue (as if it's limited only to baseball). And there are times that I agree with the fans that believe the players are out of touch with life in the real world.

But get some teens together with a Wiffle ball and a skinny yellow bat, and you will see that there is nothing wrong with the game itself. Or grab a glove and a ball and have a catch. On that holy ground you will laugh about life and bad throws and make up your own commentary for the plays taking place. It doesn't take long until your imagination is engaged and a relationship is established with everyone involved.

Passing on the love of baseball to the next generation happens one person at a time. Sometimes it's caught in the give-and-take of having a catch. Sometimes it's caught when a pitcher tosses you a ball after warming-up. Learning how to keep score, watching the dance of the defense when a ball is hit, and sharing stories of yesterday's heroes are all ways to pass on the love of the game.

For the last fourteen years, I have been involved in working with teens through churches. I'm supposed to know how to encourage them and teach them the way of faith, the way of following Jesus. I hear stories of churches with enormous budgets for youth ministry, with hundreds of youth in attendance on a weekly basis, and I am always a little jealous. For the last several years, I have operated from a zero-dollar youth budget. I get hundreds of emails and letters trying to sell me on the latest and greatest in youth ministry materials and programs. I rarely read them. I simply don't think that effective youth ministry can be packaged or purchased. When it comes to ministry, money isn't everything.

Passing on the love of Jesus to the next generation happens

one person at a time. I'm not exactly your highly-energetic-charismatic-entertainment-driven leader. In fact, I'm kind of slow and boring. We gather together and play foursquare and pray. We read Scriptures and talk about the highs and lows of our lives, trying to catch a glimpse of the holy. Once a year we go on a pilgrimage called "Youth Camp" where we center ourselves again in the Great Story of God.

My "program" is nothing fancy or flashy. It's based in hugs and smiles and the simple reminder that we follow Jesus together. My focus while working with the youth is laying a foundation for a lifelong relationship. I have been doing this "youth ministry" thing long enough now to have former youth who are parents, and I've wondered if I'll stay at this until I am sharing Jesus stories with their kids as well.

One of my favorite things is watching a youth graduate high school and being introduced not as "youth minister," but "friend." On those occasions, I know that I've been a part of something holy and sacred. In a culture and world that loves to define and label, "friend" is definitely one of my favorite labels.

People who study such things are concerned about the future of youth ministry. They talk about being effective as youth ministers and how that can be measured. They talk about this generation that is obsessed with the latest technology, and they wonder how something old and slow like Scripture can possibly be communicated. They talk about numbers and budgets and extreme experiences, and I find myself shaking my head and wondering how I would ever begin to explain my job to someone from a third-world country.

It is the responsibility of all followers of Jesus to mentor and disciple the next generation. However, "What's in it for me? What will I get out of it?" is the prevalent attitude of many adults my age who go to church. Selfishness now abounds in the place where we are taught to die to self. With that kind of attitude, no wonder "the experts" are concerned about the transmission of faith to the next generation.

* * * * *

It is not my goal to make Kaleb dislike the Yankees. I'm thrilled that he has a team he loves and is excited to watch. It was fun to watch him bounce around and dance and laugh when I gave him the ticket for the game on Easter Sunday. It is my goal to let Kaleb know that he is someone important to somebody. It's not my job to chastise him for bad grades or poor decisions. It's not my job to guilt him into going to church every time the doors are open. My job is to share life with Kaleb, and sometimes that's easier at the ballpark than at the church.

* * * * *

The Royals and the Yankees played six games against each other this season. They each won three. Maybe when it comes to church *and* baseball, money isn't everything.

18

Sacred Time

August 18, 2011
Royals' Record: 51-73
My Record: 8-7

"I played at a great time for baseball.
Shed no tears for me.
I was right on time."
—Buck O'Neil

There are two Greek words that are both defined as *time*. The first is *chronos*. *Chronos* time is time that can be measured and exists in a logical, sequential order. *Chronos* is the Greek god of time, often referred to as "Father Time." Father Time is regularly seen pictured with wings, because, as we all know, "time flies."

In the United States, we obsess about *chronos* time. We try to control time, employing numerous time-management devices to help us plan our days and hours and minutes. I have one friend who gets a new calendar every couple of months, convinced that if he can better manage his time, he will better manage his life. We love to try to manipulate time by setting our clocks fast so we can hit the snooze button more. (I *so* do this one.) We are fascinated by the concept of the space-time continuum, as it is broached on most every sci-fi show worth its salt.[44] We are always talking about the relative speed of time—how slowly it moves during the workday, yet how fast the years go by. We also talk about time in terms of quantity—if you have a surplus, you are bored, and there's never enough of it on the weekend. This is all *chronos* time.

The second Greek word for time is *kairos*. *Kairos* time is measured by quality and is sacred time that refuses to be quantified. God lives and acts and moves in *kairos* time, which rarely, if ever, coincides with our perceptions or desires for Him to act in *chronos* time. We recognize *kairos* time as those moments in our lives when it seems that time is standing still. Sometimes *kairos* moments occur when we are in nature—watching a sunrise or a sunset or a meteor shower in the mountains of Colorado. Sometimes, *kairos* moments occur when we play with children. Sometimes, *kairos* moments occur in that space between asleep and awake when we catch a glimpse of a place where time has no meaning.

* * * * *

One of my favorite things to do before a Royals game is to watch the starting pitcher warm up in the bullpen. Watching the pitcher's routine is an entrance into *kairos* time for me. I try to peek into his glove at his hands, to see how he holds pitches. I peer into the bullpen as he focuses on keeping the ball on the corners of the plate and down in the zone. And I love the nonverbal communication that takes place between him and the catcher, the flips of the glove that signal the pitch, the affirming nods, the wiggles of the hands.

---

44 Like *Eureka*.

Sacred Time 147

The starting pitcher usually begins his warm-up routine thirty minutes before the first pitch ceremonies. I coordinated schedules with Brett the Artist, Greg the Musician, and my friend Eddie in secret hopes of arriving at the stadium early enough to watch Luke Hochevar's pre-game routine. Two wrecks on the highway, however, threw a wrench into my plan. *Chronos* time marched on relentlessly, and we barely made it into our seats before the game started.

Tonight, the Royals hosted the Boston Red Sox. Founded in 1901, the Boston Red Sox are one of the charter franchises of the American League. Cy Young and Babe Ruth defined the early years of the team. Once Babe was sold to the Yankees, the "Curse of the Bambino" fell on Boston, keeping them from winning the World Series until 2004 (or so the legend goes). I've been told that fans in Boston are so knowledgeable about the game that they know more about your team than you do. I believe it.

In the bottom of the first inning, Brett the Artist informed us of an approaching storm. My friend Eddie looked up the radar screen on his phone, and we saw a large green, red, and yellow monster approaching us from the north. From our seats, we could see the edge of the storm front directly over the centerfield scoreboard. Time would be an important issue in tonight's game.

Baseball, however, is one of the few sports that is played in *kairos* time. Once the game begins, there is no pitch clock or artificial division of time that necessitates the game's ending. Theoretically, a game could last forever. The longest professional baseball game occurred at the AAA level between the Pawtucket Red Sox and the Rochester Red Wings. The game lasted 33 innings and Pawtucket won 3-2. Numerous records were set in that game which started on Holy Saturday and ended on June 23.[45]

---

[45] Unless you believe W.P. Kinsella's *The Iowa Baseball Confederacy*. If you believe

I spotted Randy the home inspector just a few rows in front of me. I walked down to visit with him for a few moments, filling him in on the house that we didn't get and the new house we would hopefully close on in the middle of the World Series. He was encouraging, saying that it's never wise to rush into a house. While visiting with Randy, I noticed Phil, one of my friends from high school.

I cannot remember the last time I saw Phil. He was one year older than me in school, and we played ball together on a couple of occasions. He is now a pastor in Springfield, an author, a speaker, and a blogger. Phil was in town with his family because the Red Sox were playing. They wore Red Sox jerseys and were cheering for Ortiz, even though he was on the disabled list. For a few minutes, leaning against the concrete wall, Phil and I reconnected, reminiscing in each other's presence. He introduced me to his kids and we shared stories of life after high school. It was another taste of *kairos* time.

Heading back up to my seats as Phil walked down to his, both Eddie and Brett talked about the storm. "It's definitely a question of whether or not we can get the innings in." Luke Hochevar, however, was not in a hurry. He took his time, catching his breath in between pitches and walking around the mound. In the post-game interview, Hochevar explained that he didn't want to rush himself. Hochevar was pitching in *kairos* time. But this was not good for eluding the storm that would be coming in a little over two hours.

Some people complain that baseball is too slow, that it is not exciting enough for the current generation. We have been trained through technology and ADHD television programming to live distractedly. Our brains whizz and whirr, constantly searching for

---

Kinsella, the AAA game is nothing.

something to think on, to ponder over, or to worry about. Maybe this comes from the large doses of caffeine, espresso, and energy drinks we consume. Maybe it comes from years of playing video games or carrying multiple cell phones just in case someone needs to get in touch with us. Maybe it is the curse of trying to keep up with the Joneses. In the end, however, *chronos* time and baseball are simply not compatible.

You can't play baseball in a hurry. You can't watch baseball in a hurry. To enjoy baseball, you must enter *kairos* time. Worries of deadlines and any other events that take place in *chronos* time must be temporarily set aside. When players step between the white lines, lean back into your seat, take a deep breath, enter into conversations, remember the teams and games of yesteryear, and simply try to be.

* * * * *

According to an article I recently read in the *New Yorker*, it is actually impossible to live in the present moment. We are always a little late, thanks to how our brains process time.[46] Our brains need to interpret the events and information coming in through our various senses. This interpretation happens in hundreds of milliseconds. We process it as being instantaneous.

If it takes time for our brains to process the present moment, doesn't it make sense that it would take our souls even longer? Most of our church worship services are tightly structured gatherings that rush to end by noon so we can get to lunch. I'm not saying that worship should be longer, which would torture my kids. I'm saying that it needs to have a touch of *kairos* time. Still,

---

46   http://www.newyorker.com/reporting/2011/04/25/110425fa_fact_bilger, accessed on May 30, 2012.

even on the one semi-sacred day of the week, we prefer to live by *chronos* time.

I am an introvert. I take a long time to process and think things through. Most of my thinking and processing happens while I write or ride my bike. However, in our extrovert-dominant society, time for reflection is not easy to find. Creating sacred space for breathing should be a high priority for those who strive to connect to the souls of others. For me, the sanctuary of Royals stadium provides space and time for my soul to renew. There are no expectations placed on me while I am at the game. I can simply sit back and watch. I can interact with other fans around me whom I don't know. I can stand and cheer and scream, dance to the music, and yell at the top of my lungs. All of the above behaviors are acceptable. All are a part of belonging to the called-out community of Royals fans.

* * * * *

The Royals' outfield continued their trend of throwing out runners, extending their major league leading number of assists. Melky Cabrera connected to rookie catcher, Salvador Perez, for a fly out, gun-'em-down-at-home double play and Alex Gordon threw out a runner at second. A piece of unsolicited advice: even if you're the Red Sox, station-to-station baseball is recommended against this Royals' outfield.

Alex Gordon doubled and scored in the first and hit a two-run homer in the third, accounting for all three of the Royals' runs. However, a two-out single by Dustin Pedroia in the top of the fifth inning gave the Red Sox a one-run lead, to which they would precariously cling for the remainder of the game.

By the end of the ninth inning, we were watching lightning

dance in the sky to the north. Rain started falling thirty minutes later as I pulled into my driveway, accompanied by howling winds. Fearful girls greeted me at the door.

* * * * *

In the book *Shoeless Joe* by W.P. Kinsella, author J.D. Salinger says, "I don't have to tell you that the one constant through all the years has been baseball. America has been erased like a blackboard, only to be rebuilt and then erased again. But baseball has marked time while America has rolled by like a procession of steamrollers."[47]

And in the movie adaptation, *Field of Dreams,* Terrance Mann finishes the soliloquy saying, "But baseball has marked the time. This field, this game—it's a part of our past, Ray. It reminds us of all that once was good and it could be again."

So go to your nearest baseball stadium, turn off your phone, and breathe. Refuse to be in a hurry. Let your soul sing as you learn to enter into *kairos* time.

---

[47] W.P. Kinsella, *Shoeless Joe* (New York: Mariner Books, 1999) pp. 252-3.

19

Weathering the Storm

September 3, 2011
Royals' Record: 57-82
My Record: 8-8

"Sometimes pain
Is better left behind.
America's a better place now.
Not perfect. But better.
We survived, man."
—Buck O'Neil

I have two friends named Kevin, both of whom attend my church. One friend is Kevin the Builder. Anything and everything related to construction is possible for Kevin the Builder. For those of you who think you already know "the builder," trust me, Bob is nothing compared to Kevin. I've even worked with Kevin the Builder on a project before: I was the go-for and clean-up crew.

My other Kevin-friend is Kevin the Musician. Now, Kevin the Builder has a beautiful bass voice; I've sung with him at youth camp for years. But Kevin the Musician formerly played piano, sang, and danced professionally in Branson. He and I have been in the worship band together for years. We've spent time in the studio, recording CD projects together, as well as time on the road, singing and performing at various venues and leading worship for other youth groups.

Kevin the Musician called me during lunch today and invited me to tonight's game. The last time he invited me to a game, we sat right behind the Royals' dugout, and I must confess, this was the first thing that popped into my mind. However, even with the possibility of ridiculously good seats, I was hesitant to say yes. I knew the forecast predicted storms and I didn't particularly want to get soaked—I melt in the rain. I narrowly avoided a soaking at the last game and didn't expect my luck to extend through this one as well. Still, for a chance at my best seats of the season, I figured I would give it a go.

A couple months earlier, Jamie was at Wal-Mart and found a blue poncho for sale. Knowing how much I dislike rain and how much I love the color blue, she bought it for a couple of bucks.

Kevin the Musician asked me to meet him at his house an hour before the game. It was pouring as I drove. I pulled up in front of his house, threw the poncho to the back seat, and asked if he still wanted to go. "Might as well give it a shot," he answered, "Nothing else is on tonight's agenda."

We drove to the stadium as the rain continued to pour. Listening to the pre-game show, we heard that the first pitch was delayed thirty minutes. We pulled into the parking lot and looked west. There appeared to be a break in the clouds, and we hoped that it would be sufficient to play the five-inning minimum for an official game. As we got out of the car, the wind picked up and the rain resumed. Kevin wrestled with his umbrella to make it cooperate—it didn't. He laughed in frustration. I put on the blue-poncho-personal-sweat-lodge. We proceeded to the gates, slipped through the turnstiles, and were awarded with a bobble-head of Joakim Soria. *Sweet.*

As the rain continued, we spent some time in the team store, commenting on the various prices of the mementos. Looking at all things blue and baseball and trying my best not to covet, I made a mental note of a couple things I'd like to get for Kaylea and Sophie before season's end. I accidentally bumped into an elderly gentleman and ended up helping him and his grandson look through a stack of game-used baseballs, hoping to find one from the date of the boy's first game. We found balls with dates earlier and later, but not on the exact game day.

Kevin and I exited the store and continued walking around the stadium. We noticed that the grounds crew had removed the tarp from the infield and was diligently working to prepare the field for play. A small lake had formed on the warning track in center field; hopefully, it wouldn't come into play. Halfway to our seats, we came across "Royal Thunder," the drum-line from Missouri Southern in Joplin. We listened to one of their pieces and cheered for them when they finished. I shook the hands of a couple of quints players and told them that they were amazing. Kevin and I spent the next few minutes dialoguing about the abilities of drummers to not only keep time, but to do different things with different parts of their bodies.

We arrived at our seats and dried them off as best we could before sitting down. Tonight we were just a few rows further back than last time. The colors were presented, the national anthem was sung, and the game began only twenty minutes late. From here, we could actually hear the players on the field talking.

The first batter blooped a ball to right field for a single. Luke

Hochevar tried to pick him off first and threw the ball away. Two batters later, Carlos Santana hit a sacrifice fly and gave the Cleveland Indians a quick 1-0 lead. In the bottom half of the inning, Jeff Francoeur drove a two-out double down the right field line, scoring Melky Cabrera and Eric Hosmer, giving the Royals the lead.

And then the rain returned.

We chose to wait, taking our chances to weather the storm.

* * * * *

I feel like I'm in the middle of a life storm, or a series of pre-midlife crises, or something like that.

I completed my Master's degree ten years ago and have barely made a dent in the debt re-payment. I make less now than I ever have, working as a part-time youth minister, freelance writer, and indie musician. I know I could go to a different church and make more money, but I deeply believe that true ministry takes place over the long haul. I don't want my youth to think that they were stepping-stones to a "better job." Sure, I enjoy preaching on occasion, but I know that I am not a very compassionate shepherd, and I have no real desire to lead a church of my own. I don't want to mess with administration and coordinating a million meetings and the feeling that there are some people who aren't happy with me.

Besides, I love the heart and vision my church has for reaching out into the community. A couple of years ago, we started our own non-profit organization, called *Coldwater*, for the express purpose of living out the love of Jesus with new friends.[48] *Coldwater* has a free food pantry and a free clothes closet. We distribute food to chronically hungry children in our local elementary schools through a back-snack program. We are in the process of build-

---

48   www.coldwater.me

ing affordable housing for low-income elderly and special-needs adults. I deeply believe that *Coldwater* is a Christ-presence in the community.

Most days, I try to simply do the work for that day. I show up and write my words. I query agents and publishers. Just last night, I received an email from an agent who said, "You are a gifted and talented writer. Unfortunately, I don't know what I could do with your writings." His advice was to keep writing. So I look for quiet places to write where people don't smack their gum or use speakerphone to hold conversations in foreign languages. I also look for places to write where people don't continuously ask to read what I'm writing. I write my words and make my sentences in hope that someday people will read them.

Jamie and I live month-to-month at best, finding creative ways to make our income cover our expenses. We don't have cable and often say "No" to the girls' requests for this, that, or the other. When, inevitably, the question about Disney World is broached, I respond with trust and hope, "I promise, we will take you there." One day, I will follow through; I just don't know when.

Every day, I wrestle with haunting questions. Did I mishear what God said? Am I doing what I'm "supposed" to be doing? Is this where I belong? Did I take a wrong turn and now I won't see the burning bush intended for me? Am I listening to the wrong voice? Am I insane? Who am I to think that my writing is good enough? Who am I to believe that these stories really matter?

I am afraid that I am preparing my girls for a lifetime of counseling, not that there's anything wrong with that. I feel like I'm living in the middle of an Old Testament story, and I have no idea how it's going to end. A couple of weeks ago, while the questions continued to bombard my brain, I grabbed my guitar and sat down to play. In a matter of moments, I penned these words:

> Looking for a better story
> Where heroes come and save the day
> Tired of chasing after glory
> Tired of facing the same old thing
>
> Waiting for some inspiration
> Paint a rainbow on these skies of gray
> Just another explanation
> Another reason to walk away
>
> Running mazes of confusion
> And I don't know which way to go
> Am I reaching for illusion?
> Or on display, my life the show
>
> I'll scream and shout
> Over ocean storm
> What difference does it make?
> I'm waiting for a miracle
> For Love to find a way
> Into this heart

There's a story in the Scriptures about Jesus, his friends, and a storm. They were out on the lake and their boat was pelted by waves, tossed around to the point where even the seasoned fishermen were afraid. Jesus was taking a nap. I sometimes wonder if Jesus is sleeping in the middle of my life storm. If so, I have no idea how to wake him up. Maybe I need to take some lessons from Lieutenant Dan and start screaming at the top of my lungs, laughing at the lightning, thrilled by the thunder.

Shortly after we were married, Jamie and I were caught in a flash flood. I was driving our "new" 1986 Honda Prelude through the streets of Springfield, Missouri, in the rain, when a river came shooting out of a storm drain, stopping our car dead in its tracks. Within seconds, water started to rise inside the car. Jamie jumped out of her window to go for help. As soon as she left, two men came over and pushed my car out of the mini-lake and got it running again. With toothless grins, they shouted, "You'll make it home okay, don't worry!" It was one of the most terrifying experiences in my life. To this day, I am not particularly fond of driving in the rain.

I have always felt that those toothless strangers were messengers from God, doing what needed to be done when I needed it the most. Sometimes, in the middle of the storm, the best thing that one can do is wait. Still, waiting is about as much fun as going to the dentist. Too often, we try to take matters into our own hands, thinking, "God helps those who help themselves," which leaves us spinning our wheels and going nowhere.[49]

How do you know when it's time to quit waiting and do something? There aren't any specialists who can look at a waiting-radar map and tell you whether you are entering or exiting the storm. Waiting is an act of faith, trusting that God is not sleeping through the storm, that prayers are not ignored, that we will again taste and see that God is good. I was reading a story in Scripture a couple of days ago and noticed that twenty-five years passed in between two verses. Nothing is written about those twenty-five years. I wondered if I could wait and persevere for twenty-five years. I hope I don't have to find out.

Waiting is not for the faint of heart and is never the time to

---

[49] This quote is NOT Scripture. Its origin lies in Ancient Greece. English political theorist, Algernon Sidney, first wrote it in our modern form almost forty years before Benjamin Franklin ever quoted it.

plea-bargain with God. "God, if you will get me that raise, I'll never miss another Sunday." Strike one. "God, just get me through this, and I'll volunteer at the shelter every month." Strike two. The third attempt at plea-bargaining will result in a foul tip. God's mercies are new every day; we don't ever strike out with God. Regardless, attempting to manipulate God through bargaining is never a wise idea.

Waiting is choosing to love God in the middle of our humanity, with all the questions and thunder reverberating within.

* * * * *

Thankfully, the rain delay in the second inning lasted only 16 minutes. As soon as possible, I took off the heat-harnessing poncho and watched as Luke Hochevar pitched a masterpiece, allowing only two more hits over the next seven innings. The Royals easily won 5-1, and Kevin the Musician and I celebrated a wonderful game.

It was worth the risk of getting soaked to drive to the stadium, bearing a towel and a blue weight-loss-inducing poncho. It was worth sitting in my own personal sauna, waiting, and listening to the symphony of the rain on my hood to witness a gem of a pitching performance.

The only certainty of trying to live a life of faith is the storms. We must remember: we are promised Presence through the storms. We are promised that the storms cannot separate us from God's love. The rainbow only appears after the storm has passed.

> Wait for the Lord.
> Be strong; take heart.
> And wait for the Lord.[50]

---
50 Psalm 27.14

20

Take a Bow

September 13, 2011
Royals' Record: 62-86
My Record: 9-8

"All we can say of him tonight is he belongs in our Hall of Fame."
—Ken Burns, talking about Buck O'Neil

I remember helping Grant the Programmer paint a bedroom while listening to *Royals on Radio* and peeking in at the broadcast on TV during breaks—Mike Sweeney had a great game that night. Grant the Programmer and his wife, Casey the Violinist, were expecting their firstborn and, thanks to a planned C-section, knew to the minute when he would arrive. Grant and I are spades partners and quite good ones when Grant pays attention to what I play. When the girls were younger, Friday nights were reserved for dinner and spades. Grant and Casey played with the girls—reading books, playing games, crafting crafts—and helped us with the adventure of getting them into bed. When we learned that Casey was pregnant, I knew beyond the shadow of a doubt that Grant would be a great dad. Thanks to technology, we learned that they would be having a boy. He would be named Colten.

In February of 2007, Colten was born at St. Mary's Hospital in Blue Springs, and immediately the doctors knew something was wrong. He was transferred by ambulance to Children's Mercy Hospital in downtown Kansas City, where he was hooked up to numerous monitors and tubes. He didn't cry. He didn't nurse. He was limp as a rag doll. The hoped-for post-partum celebration turned into a day-by-day time of prayer, waiting for the specialists to announce what was "wrong."

At some point in this period of waiting, I wrote a lullaby for Colten. I asked Casey, who has played in the worship band with me for years, if I could bring my guitar to the hospital and play my song for Colten. She escorted me back to the NICU and gently untangled Colten from a mess of cords. As I started singing, a couple of nurses gathered nearby. It was probably one of my most important concerts, for an audience of "only" four—not counting the angels in that sacred place.

In due course of time, Colten was diagnosed with Prader-Willi Syndrome (PWS). An extremely rare syndrome occurring in one out of every 20,000 births, PWS is a genetic-deletion syndrome affecting the 15th chromosome. It is characterized by low muscle tone, a reduced metabolism, and, as those affected get older, a voracious appetite. In simple terms, our bodies tell our brains when we are full, although, as a culture, we tend to ignore that signal. Colten's body simply doesn't produce that signal. If presented with the opportunity, he would eat until his stomach ruptured.

To date, there is no cure for PWS.

For the first couple years of his life, Jamie was Colten's babysitter. She tried to teach me about counting calories and portion sizes and which foods we simply could not eat in Colten's presence. My family now understands firsthand the struggles with meals and snacks, not to mention our country's obsession with unhealthy eating tendencies.

But we live in an era of hope, where every day holds the possibility of discovering a cure.

On Labor Day, my family joined Colten's extended family and other friends for a party involving wonderful food and a tour of Colten's grandpa's garden and the construction work in his basement. Something resembling a softball game, with baseballs and unlimited strikes but without base running or score keeping, broke out. After an hour's worth of chasing down fly balls and praying that the grounders wouldn't bust out a tooth, I took a break.

Colten was standing on the driveway with a glove in-hand and wanted to know if I would play catch with him. It took a couple minutes to place the too-large piece of leather on his left hand, then on his right hand, then back to his left hand and finally, back on his right hand. Standing three feet away, I stretched out my arm and dropped the ball into his mitt. Colten grabbed it, bent his arm behind his head, and threw the ball as hard as he could with his whole body. It made it to me in the air.

Colten *loves* music. He has heard Casey and me play hundreds of times, even though he is only four. Colten applied what he knew of music to baseball: instead of seeking applause after a good catch or throw, Colten bowed. Whenever I threw him the ball, Colten said, "Take a bow, Ethan. Take a bow." He would not throw the ball back until after I bowed.

I had never bowed playing baseball. Until then. Lifting my

arms up high, I bowed as deeply as physically possible. Colten cheered and threw me the ball.

* * * * *

The end of the season is near. After tonight there are only thirteen games left, as the Royals will not be playing in the postseason. On my last couple of trips to Chick-fil-A, I have asked to talk to Jake, to break the bad news. I have yet to see him.

Grant the Programmer and I entered the stadium early enough to partake of the last "T-Shirt Tuesday" offerings, and we both sported new, white, long-sleeve shirts with the Royals emblem on the front by evening's end. There was a taste of fall in the air, and come the later innings, the extra layer felt good.

Tonight's game was for pride. A victory tonight would guarantee that the Royals' would not lose 100 games this season. A victory tonight would also keep the Royals out of last place in their division. The Royals have been playing good ball in recent weeks, and tonight was no exception. Bruce Chen gave up two hits in eight scoreless innings pitched. And Alex Gordon put up an impressive line—three hits, one homerun, and two RBI's.

Alex led off the bottom of the third inning with a long home run. The stadium thundered. I must have been inspired sitting next to Grant because my first thought was, *Take a bow, Alex.* I am now officially campaigning for Alex Gordon to win the MVP award for the American League.

In reality, I know that Alex doesn't stand a chance to be voted as MVP, though he should definitely be a frontrunner. It's hard to be an MVP on a losing team. It's even harder to be an MVP on a losing team in the Midwest. In order to win the award, Alex will be compared to every other superstar on every other team, especially the coastal teams. He has played near-errorless ball in left field and leads the majors in outfield assists. With a little luck over the final couple of weeks, he will hit over .300 and post his best numbers in every offensive category, including home runs, stolen bases, RBI, doubles—you name it. However, a cursory search of "American League MVP" online reveals that Gordon's name isn't even listed as an honorable mention.

When we read Scripture, we often point out the numerous MVPs of faith, propping them up on pedestals, trying to live like them. Many people refer to Hebrews 11 as the "Faith Hall of Fame," which I don't think is fair to the rest of us. Not that I begin to qualify to be included in that list, but there's a part of me that is always comparing myself with what little I know of my faith predecessors through their stories.

Comparing myself to others is a dangerous exercise. In the sports world, numbers are used for everything. But towards the end of Galatians, Paul writes this:

> Make a careful exploration of who you are and the work you have been given, and then sink yourself into that. Don't be impressed with yourself. Don't compare yourself with others. Each of you must take responsibility for doing the creative best you can with your own life.[51]

Part of the struggle of living in a consumerist culture is our obsession and drive to compare apples to oranges to organically grown cell phones. We compare so we can hand out our prestigious awards—valedictorian, *magna cum laude*, Rhodes scholar, New York Times best-selling author—and so we can order our top-ten lists.

Maybe our desire to find persons worthy of such prestigious

---

51 Galatians 6.4-5 (MSG). I dare you to quote that verse at your next performance review.

awards comes from our hope to discover extraordinary heroes living among us—individuals of remarkable strength, ridiculous intellect, and selfless character. My experience tells me that there are people like that in this world, but our gate-keeping-dollar-driven media will never find them. The real heroes live and serve behind the scenes. They don't seek attention or fame. They simply look at their corner in this world and strive to be a light and source of hope.

*****

Toward the end of the game, Grant the Programmer and I were watching from near the fountains, having already decided to leave in the top of the ninth inning. Walking to the gates, we heard a little boy yelling, "Dad, where are you? I can't find you." We watched for a minute, waiting to see if "Dad" would appear. Grant walked over to the boy and asked, "Are you lost? Do you know where your Dad is?"

The boy told us his name and we introduced him to a Royals' Event Staff person wearing headphones. The boy said that he was five and described Dad as being older and taller and someone who might have some gray hair, but without a tattoo on his nose. (I prompted that last detail.) The search for Dad lasted the entire ninth inning. As the fireworks were blasting off overhead and the crowd of twenty-five thousand plus were celebrating the shutout victory, a second Event Staff person appeared and directed the boy around the concourse toward Dad. Dad lowered himself to his knees, and the boy ran and jumped into Dad's arms. Immediately, my eyes started watering and I choked up.

Grant leaned over to me and said, "Just think if that had been Colten. With his speech difficulties, it would have been a nightmare." We never introduced ourselves to Dad and, after witnessing the Hollywood ending, Grant and I headed for the car and for home. Grant was tonight's MVP.

Take a bow, Grant.

* * * * *

When I got home, I went straight for the girls' room. They were both asleep; Kaylea was snoring. I leaned over to kiss them both, humbly whispering prayers of thanks for these two amazing little persons who love and trust and play with me.

I know that, if I had had a little boy, I would have secretly or not-so-secretly held onto major league dreams for him. I refuse to say that the chances are impossible, but even for me, it is hard to imagine Colten playing ball professionally. So whether it's at his house or mine or the lawn of the church, any time he wants to play catch, I'll be honored.

Even if I have to take a bow.

21

Run Home

September 15, 2011
Royals' Record: 64-86
My Record: 10-8

> *"I gotta get back*
> *To Swope Park,*
> *Put my tee in the ground,*
> *Hear Swope say,*
> *"Where you been, Buck?"*
> *I say, "Been all over."*
> *And Swope will tell me,*
> *"You know better than that.*
> *Come on home."*
> —Buck O'Neil

I put a deposit on a rental house today. This is the same house that Jamie found and Randy inspected just a couple of months ago. The deal collapsed the day before closing. In the last couple of months, someone else bought the house and did all the necessary repair work. Now it is on the market for rent. Before the World Series is over, the house I once tried to buy will be the place my family calls home.

Home is a difficult and interesting concept. Home is as much about knowing one's place as it is about knowing oneself. I was born in Columbia, Missouri, and moved to Lee's Summit, Missouri; Grand Junction, Colorado; and Springfield, Missouri, all before second grade. I stayed in Springfield from second grade until I obtained my Bachelor's degree. Then Jamie and I moved to Waco, Texas, to get my Master's degree. Upon graduation from seminary, I returned to Lee's Summit, where I have been employed at Cornerstone Church for the last ten years. However, when I hear the word "home," I still think of Springfield. I think of Andy's Frozen Custard, cashew chicken, Kickapoo High School, and the Ben-Hogan/Nike Tour at Highland Springs Country Club.

For the last year, my family has shared a house with the Mueller family—Jake, Jen, and Gabe. I first met Jake at Doozen's Coffee Shop, and I gave him a hard time because he carried a fat Bible. It was a study Bible of some kind and I'm biased against study Bibles. One of my friends always says, "The Holy-Spirit-inspired footnotes told me exactly what this passage means." It seems to me that fat Bibles, which are supposed to encourage deeper thinking processes, actually prohibit us from slowing down and pondering the text on our own, from listening to the fresh wind of the Spirit. But I could be wrong.

So I teased Jake about his fat Bible and asked what he was reading. Over the next few months, we emailed and texted and talked at Doozen's, and to make a ridiculously long and convoluted story short, my family ended up moving into his house in August of 2010. My aunts and uncles and grandmas thought that I had lost my mind. (This is still a possibility.) They couldn't understand why we would voluntarily move out of our house and into the basement of someone else's house. My only answer was, "We are learning how to share life together and help one another out."

Both girls immediately loved the new home. Sophie was thrilled to have a "baby brother" in Gabe, Jake's one-year-old son. Kaylea loved having numerous friends nearby and roamed the neighborhood on her bicycle. Jamie liked sharing responsibilities for meals and eating together on a regular basis. I felt completely overwhelmed. Jake's house did not "feel" like home to me. I just wanted to get a peaceful night's sleep. It took me a couple of months to work through the transitions and develop new routines. Over the last year, I've learned a lot about what home really is.

* * * * *

Tonight, my family went to the game with Tessa and Andy and their two children, Alivia and Drew. Tessa's parents live just across the street from our old house, and we've been friends for years. Now Sophie and Alivia are in the same first-grade class, as Tessa and Andy live just a couple of blocks away from Jake's house. Tessa was Gabe's first baby-sitter. (Did you follow all of that?)

My family got to the game just a little late, waiting for Sophie's ballet class to end. We settled into our seats in the middle of the first inning, and Sophie prompted Alivia to ask me her standard question, "Are we going to see fireworks tonight?"

"If there's a home run, kiddo."

The Royals' hitters continued their September hot streak, putting runners on base every inning. However, after five-and-a-half innings, the Royals were only leading by one run, rain was starting to fall, and the temperature was rapidly dropping. In the bottom of the sixth, Drew climbed up in my lap, mainly because I was sitting closest to the Twizzlers and pretzels. Alex Gordon led off the inning with a walk and Melky Cabrera doubled him to third base. Billy Butler stepped up to the plate, and on the second pitch he blasted a three-run home run to left-center field. I picked Drew up and started cheering, "Woo hoo! Way to go Billy! Home run! Fireworks! Yea!"

Drew was surprised at my outburst. With eyes as big as baseballs, he mimicked my response, "Yeah! Go Billy! Fireworks! Run home!"

As fireworks lit up the night sky, I was immediately reminded of the movie *Hook*, starring Dustin Hoffman and Robin Williams. Hoffman, playing the manipulative Captain Hook, kidnaps Peter Pan's children and takes them to Neverland. Hook's hope is for one final, epic battle with Peter Pan. Jack, Pan's son, is angry at his father for always missing his baseball games, so Hook organizes a game just for Jack, to finally win the boy's loyalty over his father. When Jack steps up to the plate, the pirates in the stands—who know nothing of baseball—hold up signs and start chanting, "Run home, Jack! Run home, Jack!" And, for a brief moment, Jack remembers whose son he really is, and that his home is not Neverland.[52]

In that moment of celebration, with Drew in my arms, I started thinking about the power of the place we call home.

* * * * *

Can we begin to truly know ourselves if we don't have a place we call home?

---

[52] Adam Thomas is another theologian who used this same scene to talk about home here: http://wherethewind.com/2009/01/04/run-home-jack/.

Every spring for the last several years, my family has participated in Hillcrest's Walk for the Homeless. Hillcrest Transitional Housing is a "90-day transitional housing program that helps a homeless family achieve self-sufficiency through a high accountability budgeting and life skills educational curriculum while living in a fully furnished, rent-free apartment."[53] Families that enter the program have over a 95-percent chance of being self-sufficient upon graduating the program and over an 80-percent chance of remaining self-sufficient after 5 years.

Several years ago, in the weeks leading up to the walk, Kaylea started asking me some questions about the event.

"Dad, how does walking help homeless people?"

"Dad, if I ride my bike, does it still help them?"

"Dad, will there be doughnuts again?"

I told her that the walk is to show our support for what Hillcrest is doing and to make new friends with the residents. I told her that I ask grandparents and other family members for small donations and then write a check to Hillcrest to help those in the program. Kaylea then surprised me by her response.

"Dad, I'd like to raise my own money to help friends find homes."

I asked her how she planned to do it.

"Well, I like to draw, so I'll draw pictures and sell them for a dollar and give all the money I make to Hillcrest. Do you think I can raise $50 selling pictures?"

"Sure," I replied hopefully, although I had strong doubts.

Every day after school, Kaylea came home and drew three to five pictures for her "art portfolio." I didn't even know she knew what a portfolio was. I started spreading the word to friends and family members. I quickly discovered that marketing was not my gift.

---

53 www.hillcresttransitionalhousing.org, accessed September, 2011.

At that time, a local coffee shop was looking for live musicians. I had played at this venue on a couple of occasions, and I went to speak to the owner about a benefit concert and fundraiser. They were excited to partner with Kaylea.

On the evening of the fundraiser, Kaylea dressed up in her black dress, fixed her hair, and loaded up her crayons, markers, and portfolio pictures. With the help of Jared on the djembe and Casey the Violinist, I played guitar and sang for a couple of hours. There was a consistent stream of traffic through the coffee shop, especially in the room where Kaylea set up her portfolio. By evening's end, Kaylea had raised more than $500 to give to help friends find homes. She was beaming!

Not too long after this experience, I wrote a song exploring what it means to come home.

Living wanderlustfully
Chasing whim and breeze
Looking for a place that's free
Of fear and expectation

I'm passing me and waving 'hi'
I never want to say 'good-bye'
I'm haunted by the question 'why'
Still seeking affirmation

Worn down from the struggle
Lost another bout
Tired of trying to juggle
Reckless faith and nagging doubt

Coming home where the memories
Are dancing on the walls
Coming home where laughter's chasing
Footsteps down the hall
Coming home where healing love will
Kiss me when I fall
Oh, I'm coming home.

I once read that "Home is the one place we are all desperate to leave when we're young, only to long to return there the remainder of our lives."[54] When I was in high school I had dreams of going to colleges all over the country. However, when I went to Texas for seminary, all I could think about was coming back home.

Kaylea now shares my love of music. Just a couple of weeks ago, she introduced me to a song by Carrie Underwood called "Temporary Home." In the chorus we hear:

This is my temporary home
It's not where I belong.
Windows and rooms that
I'm passin' through.
This was just a stop,
On the way to where I'm going.
I'm not afraid because I know
This is my temporary home.[55]

Maybe if we lived with a sharper perspective of the temporary nature of this home, we'd be less driven to accumulate stuff for

---
54 I have no idea where I read this, but really want to give the author the proper credit. Dear Author, I'm sorry I can't find your wonderful quote at this time.
55 Carrie Underwood, "Temporary Home."

ourselves and more willing to open doors and basements, learning how to share life together.

* * * * *

St. Augustine of Hippo wrote, "*You have made us for yourself, O Lord, and our hearts are restless until they rest in you.*"[56] To me, another way of saying this is, "Our hearts are homeless until they find their home in you."

Jesus once said, "Foxes have dens and birds have nests, but the Son of Man has no place to lay his head."[57] Jesus knows what it is like to be homeless. Or, maybe, Jesus knows what it is like to be at home wherever he is. Living in the fullness of the community and kingdom of God, Jesus shared life in such a way that we might find our home with God, that we might follow him on the way Home.

When my heart finds its home in God, then and only then am I truly free. Any place where I am comfortable enough to take a nap I can now call home.

* * * * *

Billy's home run in the sixth inning put the Royals on top 6-2. They would tack on one more run in the seventh, easily beating the White Sox on this crisp autumn eve.

Baseball is ultimately about running home, crossing the plate, and celebrating with teammates a successful trip around the bases.

Life, too, is ultimately about running home, joining the celebration of the witnesses who preceded us into the Father's arms.

---

56 http://www.chinstitute.org/index.php/in-context/augustine, accessed on March 20, 2012.
57 Luke 9.58 (NIV)

In a couple of weeks, I'll be sharing a new temporary home with Jamie, Kaylea, and Sophie. It is my deepest hope that wherever we choose to live, we will dare to live boldly and fearlessly, for our hearts are running hard to find a home in God's love.

22

Save the Best for Last

September 20, 2011
Royals' Record: 67-87
My Record: 11-8

"You ought to go see a ballgame . . . Do your heart good. Help you get young."
—Buck O'Neil

I woke up this morning in a fog of melancholy, for tonight would be my last Royals game for this season. The last pair of tickets that Dad gave me for Christmas sat alone on top of my desk, next to Frank White's autograph and the ball from Opening Day. The Royals' final home game is actually tomorrow evening, but I will be busy youth minister-ing. I'll have to finish the season by listening to Denny on the radio.

I had planned to take Jamie to tonight's game as a fun date. Our last date was at a game a couple of months ago. Sometimes, though, life gets in the way of those people most precious to us. Yesterday, our babysitter texted me and cancelled with some lame excuse—her sister would be giving birth today. Likely story. All of my attempts to find another babysitter fell through. We talked with the girls and decided Kaylea could join me at tonight's game instead.

Kaylea and I left home early to stop at Chick-fil-A for dinner and hopefully make it to the stadium in time to watch some of batting practice. At Chick-fil-A, we delivered a Royals care package to Chick-fil-A Jake—a random collection of promotional propaganda acquired throughout the season. We ate and laughed and gave thanks for the food and the picture-perfect evening.

On the drive to the stadium, Kaylea's typical question barrage began, starting with, "Does Sluggerrr ever come to our seats?" I told her that I had yet to see him at our seats this year, but we could always walk to him if she wanted to. I knew Sluggerrr's assistant, Andrew Johnson, who is now the mascot for the Missouri Mavericks hockey team. Maybe we could find Andrew and give Sluggerrr a high-five or something.

"Dad, even though you've been to a lot of games, do you still get excited about going to watch the Royals play?"

The truth: on days when I know I'm going to a Royals game, I feel like a kid waiting for Christmas. I want to get to the stadium as soon as the gates open and stay through the last out, even if the Royals don't stand a chance of winning. I want to chase down batting practice balls and cheer the relief pitchers as they enter the bullpen and spend a couple of hours without worrying about "real" life. I want to see something amazing happen on the field and scream at the top of my lungs, exchanging high-fives with complete strangers when the Royals do something awesome. I looked at Kaylea and simply said, "Yep, kiddo, I still get excited."

We entered the stadium about an hour before first pitch. The Detroit Tigers, winners of the Central Division, were taking batting practice. Kaylea and I made our way to the standing-room-only seats in front of the right field fountains, hoping for a batting practice home run ball. However, in the time that we were there, not one ball cleared the fence. On the last pitch of batting practice, the hitter lined a ball to right-center field. I have learned that during batting practice it is the responsibility of pitchers to shag balls and throw them back to the infield. They have trained themselves to tune out the pleas and cries of the kids screaming for a ball. For some odd reason, on this particular hit, Tigers ace Justin Verlander fielded the ball, turned around, pointed to me, and launched it. He was far enough away that I had time to think, *I had better not drop this. Uh-oh, this might sting.* I caught the ball without a glove or a bobble. The fans on either side of us applauded.

After batting practice, Kaylea and I walked toward the Royals' bullpen so we could watch Luis Mendoza prepare for tonight's game. On the way, we stopped at the gift shop and purchased a puffy foam finger for Sophie. Ever since our first game together, Sophie has wanted a puffy finger. Tonight, I had a little extra cash and could afford the luxury, a tangible reminder of this sacred season.

Leaning on the rail, Kaylea and I watched the coaches in the bullpen prepare the mound for the warm-ups. One of them waved to us; Kaylea waved and smiled back. He nodded his head at me and flipped up a ball for me to give to Kaylea. "Dad," she said, "You can keep the ball from the Tigers' player, I want the one from the Royals' player." Mendoza and Perez warmed up, and the movement and speed of the pitches mesmerized Kaylea and me.

We made our way to our seats—section 412, row BB—right above the "Bounce" tunnel. Seated next to us was an elderly couple who said that we looked like real fans who knew a lot about baseball. We both smiled and said that we had been to quite a few games this summer. In the bottom of the first inning, the woman asked, "What about this guy, Alex Gordon? Can he just hit a home run and give us the lead?" I told her that I had seen him hit a couple of leadoff home runs this season. Then, on a full count, Alex drilled the ball 414 feet to straightaway center field. Fireworks exploded and the woman started jumping up and down, clapping and giving high-fives to all of us nearby strangers.

* * * * *

There were a couple parts of me that didn't want to come to tonight's game. One part didn't want to come because I didn't want the season to end. As long as I saw a pair of tickets on my desk, I knew that I would be attending another game. Going to watch the Royals this year has been a needed time of refuge and retreat in the midst of a summer full of stress. Even when the Royals lost, the game was a wonderful experience. Turning in my last pair of tickets would be an admission to the coming of winter and of snow, the end of this project, and six more months of waiting until Opening Day.

Another part of me was wondering just how many more stories about the intersection of baseball and faith could possibly be out there. So far, I have been to nineteen games, nineteen different, beautiful stories. What if I went to the game and couldn't find the story? What if I had to leave the game too early (it is a school night, after all) and actually missed the story? What if I witnessed a "repeat" story? Does that mean I'm still learning that particular lesson and need to focus on it again?

One of my favorite Scriptures is Matthew 6.33. When I was taking Greek in seminary I did my own translation of the verse. I rendered it: "Seek first God's Great Story and His Justice, and

God will take care of everything else." One day, my story and my stories will cease to be written. They will be swept up and completed by the Author and Perfecter of my faith. But God's Great Story never stops. It crosses all cultures and all time. And God's Great Story is the best. No more pain, no more brokenness, no more suffering. In it, God takes the harmonies and dissonances of our individual stories, orchestrating them into His divine symphony.

Tonight, Kaylea and I heard the story of a man who went to all kinds of extremes to get the autographs of this season's Royals team on his hat. Melky Cabrera was the one signature he was missing. The hat was a beautiful piece of artwork.

We listened to the stories of Aaron the Manager's latest heroics on the softball diamond, as well as the stresses of the transition from baseball season to football season. He also bought us a couple of snacks, including a souvenir soda cup, which now sits on my desk where my tickets once rested.

I overheard the story a dad shared with his son, watching the wonder grow in the son's eyes as he listened to his father. If I understood correctly, it was the boy's first game, and the dad was sharing stories from his own first game, many, many years ago.

I texted Benson the Author and told him that I was at my last game for the season and taking my oldest daughter with me. He responded, "Superior parenting skills on display," wonderful words of affirmation to one who feels more lost than found on the parenting journey.

And then Kaylea and I watched with delight as the story of the game unfolded. Eric Hosmer and Salvador Perez both had perfect nights at the plate. In fact, almost everyone in the starting lineup got a hit, with the only exception being DH Mitch Maier, who walked twice and scored two runs.

For the first time all season, Sluggerrr came up to our seats, and Kaylea joined the mob of kids hugging and high-fiving the boisterous mascot. Andrew waved at me as he tried to corral the herd of children and protect the person within the costume.

In the top of the sixth inning, the Tigers mounted a small rally, only to be squashed by a beautiful all-rookie around-the-horn double play—Moustakas to Giavotella to Hosmer. I so love the dance of a double play.

Gordon and Hosmer and Perez each hit a home run for the Royals—oh, my.

To end the game, Blake Wood struck out the last hitter, sealing the 10-2 victory.

The weather was wonderful. The defense flashed gems on numerous occasions, throwing out base runners and crashing into fences to catch deep drives. A crescendo ran throughout the entire game, building up to a beautiful ending which left my soul shouting for the entire ride home. It was, by all practical purposes, a perfect game, a fitting tribute to the Author of the Great Story, a worthy harmony for His Great Symphony.

* * * * *

Tonight's "last" game just might have been the best of the season. There was plenty of excitement and drama, plenty to cheer for and celebrate, and more than a couple unexpected gifts and surprises.

It's the same with God's Great Story. He is the first Whisper and the final Word, and our stories of brokenness and despair find their healing and completion in his love, grace, and hope. In God's Story, our stories find their meaning and their direction. The Way gets better as we walk, even through the valleys and shadows and house-buying dramas of life. The Spirit encourages us in numerous ways, giving us more than adequate strength for the day. We join our stories with others, new friends and old, and discover that a life shared is a life lived, with plenty of unexpected gifts and surprises along the way.

* * * * *

Our babysitter's sister did, in fact, have a baby while I was at the game. I went to the hospital with the hopes of holding the newborn and praying for her. Allie May was born healthy and happy. I entered the maternity ward and passed all the security tests. When I reached the door, there was a sign saying, "Do not disturb. Mother and baby resting." Staring at the sign, I whispered a blessing:

May God's face shine on you and may His grace keep you.
May you live in wonder and love without fear.
May his peace surround you as you sleep.
May you lose your story in the middle of God's Great Story.
Amen.

23

Box Scores

*"People say baseball's dead. Baseball doesn't die.
People die. Baseball lives on."*
—Buck O'Neil

Alex Gordon won his first Gold Glove Award for his stellar play in left field. He also finished 21st in the voting for the American League MVP with three points. *Take a bow, Alex.*

Eric Hosmer finished third in the voting for AL Rookie of the Year, despite leading all rookies in almost every offensive category. Sometimes it's not fair playing in the Midwest and being slighted by coastal baseball writers.

Kaylea's first fast-pitch softball season ended when she grounded out to the pitcher. She got a trophy and a medal that now sit on top of her dresser, next to the ball we acquired at our last game together. Next summer, she's considering taking horse-riding lessons.

Sophie is crafting every chance she gets. She attended "Gourd Art Camp" and made me a Royals bowl that sits on my desk. She also recently finished a project using colored construction paper detailing the Royals emblem and ballpark fireworks.

A certain "other" team from Missouri went on a terrific end-of-the-season run and won the World Series. I'm pretty sure I could hear the screams of the very vocal red team fans, but no worries; my heart is okay. I actually had a ticket to go to game seven in St. Louis, but had to sell it at the last minute.

Months ago, on Opening Day, standing by the left field foul pole with Dad and watching the George Brett interview, I heard a whisper, "Write these stories." Immediately, I knew what the Voice was asking me to do—to write the stories of this season's games, looking for glimpses of the sacred in the middle of the sport. I responded like any "normal" person would; I frowned and thought, *Leave me alone.*

Thankfully—mercifully—the Voice gave me a second chance. That evening, while at dinner with Dad and my family, the whisper came again, "Write these stories." At that moment I knew that I was on holy ground. The next day, I started writing this book.

At first, I didn't know why I was to write these stories. Part of me hoped that it would somehow result in a generous amount of money coming my way, along with an opportunity to make friends with current Royals players. Part of me thought that, maybe, I would witness the miraculous—the Royals would win the World Series, or at least make it into the postseason—and I would have a first-hand account of the season from a unique vantage point.

Upon further reflection, I think I was supposed to write these stories for three people. The first two are Kaylea and Sophie. Though they lived many of the stories, I am certain that they will forget them in years to come with more important issues of Disney World, dating, and driving weighing heavily on their hearts and minds. These stories provide a glimpse into those things I believe most deeply, yet find myself struggling to communicate clearly on a daily basis. It is my hope that they will read these stories and remember not only my love for the Royals, but also more truly, my love for them.

The third person for whom I was to write these stories was myself. In the middle of a summer of great stress and uncertainty, these stories reminded me of God's faithful presence in things big and small. They are my pillars of cloud and fire. God used this season at The K to rejuvenate my spirit, speaking through the great game of baseball to share insights about His Greater Story. Writing these stories has made me slow down, think, remember, and reflect.

In his fantastic book, *Walden,* Henry David Thoreau wrote, "I went to the woods because I wished to live deliberately, to front only the essential facts of life, and see if I could not learn what it had to teach, and not, when I came to die, discover that I had not lived."[58] Maybe my time at The K this season was to help me learn what it truly means to fully live, to "suck out all the marrow of life."[59]

Sometimes, working within the walls of the church, my perspective gets skewed. Overwhelmed by the tremendous injustices I see around the world, I despair and wonder what difference I can possibly make. I feel guilty when I consider how I have been blessed and even guiltier when I see how I take my blessings for granted.

I was sitting at Doozen's Coffee Shop finishing this book when a friend asked me what I was writing. I shared with him the basic concept of the book along with brief summaries of some of the chapters. He responded, "Isn't it amazing how God speaks to each of us in a different way, so we can hear Him? Thanks for sharing these stories; you have inspired me."

May these simple stories of life, faith, and baseball remind

---
58 Henry David Thoreau, *Walden* (New York: Oxford University Press, 2008) p. 83.
59 Ibid.

you that God is still writing His Story through all of us, each and every day.

I cannot wait to see what stories God will write through this team next season.

There has never been a better time to be a Royals fan.[60]

---

[60] One week before the beginning of the 2012 regular season, Alex Gordon signed a four-year contract extension, solidifying himself as a Royal for years to come. Take a bow, Alex.

Acknowledgments

Special thanks to the following people who lived these stories and helped make this project come to life.

Jamie, Kaylea, & Sophie Bryan
Dad & Mom
Randy Adams
Andy, Tessa, Alivia, & Drew Addleman
Robert Benson
Byron Borger
Becca Brooks
Mary Kate Brooks
Mike DeVries
Eddie Garlich
Alex Gordon
Nash High
Greg Janssen
Kevin Kelley
Brett Kesinger
Mike King
Marty Krigbaum
Aaron Mears
Kaleb Miller
Les Norman
Buck O'Neil
Katy & Joseph Oswalt
Joe Posnanski
Kevin Seitzer
Grant Shields

The entire 2011 Kansas City Royals Team